D0815544

Presented to

_____

on

_____

by

_____

_____

*Look, children are gift of the LORD, and
the fruit of the womb is a reward.*
PSALM 127:3

SPIRITLED PROMISES FOR

Moms

PASSIO
THE ART OF AUTHENTIC FAITH

MEV
MODERN
ENGLISH
VERSION

Most CHARISMA HOUSE BOOK GROUP products are available at special quantity discounts for bulk purchase for sales promotions, premiums, fund-raising, and educational needs. For details, write Charisma House Book Group, 600 Rinehart Road, Lake Mary, Florida 32746, or telephone (407) 333-0600.

SPIRITLED PROMISES FOR MOMS
Published by Passio
Charisma Media/Charisma House Book Group
600 Rinehart Road
Lake Mary, Florida 32746
www.charismahouse.com

Cover design by Lisa Rae McClure
Design Director: Justin Evans

Visit the Passio and Modern English Version websites: www.passiofaith.com and www.mevbible.com.

Library of Congress Control Number: 2014956908
International Standard Book Number: 978-1-62998-224-3
E-book ISBN: 978-1-62998-247-2
First edition
15 16 17 18 19 — 987654321
Printed in the United States of America

We are women, and my plea is let me be a woman, holy through and through, asking for nothing but what God wants to give me, receiving with both hands and with all my heart whatever that is.

ELISABETH ELLIOT

Contents

INTRODUCTION

I cannot tell you how much I owe to the
solemn word of my good mother.
—CHARLES SPURGEON

The impression that a praying mother
leaves upon her children is life-long.
—D. L. MOODY

A s a mom you spend a lot of time making sure others are comforted. But when it's time for you to have your own needs met, where do you go to be comforted? You need only to place your trust in God's strong and capable hands, relying on His promises that are established in His Word. God will never fail you.

God promises to keep you mindful of His words, but for Him to remind you, you need to know what He has said. As you soak in the wisdom of God's Word and let it breathe life into your inner spirit, you can discover renewed joy and delight for being the mom God has called you to be. By meditating on and applying God's promises, you'll learn to nurture and guide your children to a life of faith and Christian growth as you prepare them for adulthood. When you apply His promises to the issues of life that bring challenge or questions, you'll experience His promises replenishing your deepest felt needs with the strength and assurance you long for.

SpiritLed Promises for Moms will nourish and replenish your heart, mind, and soul. You'll experience your spirit being soothed with comforting scriptures from God's Word. These are specially selected promises for two hundred important life topics that renew your strength, hope, comfort, and confidence for everything that life delivers. Apply each scripture personally, and you'll experience the power of God's Word in action. You'll realize the joy in celebrating victories in many areas of your life when you learn to trust God to meet your every need.

Today's moms lead busier, faster-paced lives. You're always there for your family. There's no place you would rather be, because you know that being a mom is a special blessing and an important calling for raising your children God's way. Because you *are* "the mom" you must care for your children and your family in many ways, despite more demand on your time and attention. Faith in the wisdom found in God's promises will help you fulfill your roles in the face of these changes and allows her to prepare well for whatever comes.

SpiritLed Promises for Moms reveals the heart of the

eternal God and every promise is personal to you. By spending just a few minutes during the quiet times of your day, you'll find that God still speaks anew through the words of the Bible today—even through verses you've read many times before. Your eyes will be open to the truth in a way that frees you from things that pull you down, such as jealousy, anger, hurt, and strife. Allow God's promises to plant seeds of hope that grow into what the Bible calls the fruit of the Spirit— love, joy, peace, patience, gentleness, goodness, faith, meekness, and self-control. As you read, you'll discover how frequently a promise from the Scriptures can offer insight and answers that turn a situation around in an instant. These promises can bring key insights and develop the strength you need to reach out to your family.

God is faithful and will never let you down. He is there for you today, tomorrow, and all the days that follow. Don't be afraid to embrace His promises and reach out for comfort to your every need.

Strength and honor are her clothing, and she will rejoice in time to come. She opens her mouth with wisdom, and in her tongue is the teaching of kindness. She looks well to the ways of her household, and does not eat the bread of idleness. Her children rise up and call her blessed; her husband also, and he praises her: "Many daughters have done virtuously, but you excel them all." Charm is deceitful, and beauty is vain, but a woman who fears the LORD, she shall be praised.

—*Proverbs 31:25–30*

ACCEPTING OTHERS

Give to him who asks you, and from him who would borrow from you do not turn away. You have heard that it was said, "You shall love your neighbor and hate your enemy." But I say to you, love your enemies, bless those who curse you, do good to those who hate you, and pray for those who spitefully use you and persecute you.

—MATTHEW 5:42–44

He who receives you receives Me, and he who receives Me receives Him who sent Me.

—MATTHEW 10:40

Truly I say to you, whoever gives you a cup of water to drink in My name, because you belong to Christ, will not lose his reward.

—MARK 9:41

To love Him with all the heart, and with all the understanding, and with all the soul, and with all the strength, and to love one's neighbor as oneself, is more than all burnt offerings and sacrifices.

—MARK 12:33

Do unto others as you would have others do unto you.

—LUKE 6:31

ACCOUNTABILITY

He told His disciples: "There was a rich man who had a steward who was accused to the man of wasting his resources. So he called him and said, 'How is it that I hear this about you? Give an account of your stewardship, for you may no longer be steward.'"

—Luke 16:1–2

So then each of us shall give an account of himself to God.

—Romans 14:12

For we must all appear before the judgment seat of Christ, that each one may receive his recompense in the body, according to what he has done, whether it was good or bad.

—2 Corinthians 5:10

Providing for honest things, not only in the sight of the Lord but also in the sight of men.

—2 Corinthians 8:21

Obey your leaders and submit to them, for they watch over your souls as those who must give an account. Let them do this with joy and not complaining, for that would not be profitable to you.

—Hebrews 13:17

ADULTERY

But whoever commits adultery with a woman lacks understanding; he who does it destroys his own soul.

—Proverbs 6:32

You have heard that it was said by the ancients, "You shall not commit adultery." But I say to you that whoever looks on a woman to lust after her has committed adultery with her already in his heart.

—Matthew 5:27–28

For out of the heart proceed evil thoughts, murders, adulteries, sexual immorality, thefts, false witness, and blasphemies.

—Matthew 15:19

And if a woman divorces her husband and marries another, she commits adultery.

—Mark 10:12

Marriage is to be honored among everyone, and the bed undefiled. But God will judge the sexually immoral and adulterers.

—Hebrews 13:4

AMBITION

But seek first the kingdom of God and His righteousness, and all these things shall be given to you.

—Matthew 6:33

For what does it profit a man if he gains the whole world, yet loses or forfeits himself?

—Luke 9:25

Let nothing be done out of strife or conceit, but in humility let each esteem the other better than himself.

—Philippians 2:3

Learn to be calm, and to conduct your own business, and to work with your own hands, as we commanded you, so that you may walk honestly toward those who are outsiders and that you may lack nothing.

—1 Thessalonians 4:11–12

For where there is envying and strife, there is confusion and every evil work.

—James 3:16

ANGER

For His anger endures but a moment, in His favor is life; weeping may endure for a night, but joy comes in the morning.

—Psalm 30:5

The Lord is gracious and full of compassion, slow to anger, and great in mercy.

—Psalm 145:8

He who is slow to anger is better than the mighty, and he who rules his spirit than he who takes a city.

—Proverbs 16:32

Beloved, do not avenge yourselves, but rather give place to God's wrath, for it is written: "Vengeance is Mine. I will repay," says the Lord. Therefore "If your enemy is hungry, feed him; if he is thirsty, give him a drink; for in doing so you will heap coals of fire on his head." Do not be overcome by evil, but overcome evil with good.

—Romans 12:19–21

Love suffers long and is kind; love envies not; love flaunts not itself and is not puffed up, does not behave itself improperly, seeks not its own, is not easily provoked, thinks no evil.

—1 Corinthians 13:4–5

ANOINTING

He gives great deliverance to His king, and shows lovingkindness to His anointed, to David and to his descendants for evermore.

—Psalm 18:50

The Spirit of the Lord is upon Me, because He has anointed Me to preach the gospel to the poor; He has sent Me to heal the broken-hearted, to preach deliverance to the captives and recovery of sight to the blind, to set at liberty those who are oppressed.

—Luke 4:18

I thank Christ Jesus our Lord, who has enabled me, because He counted me faithful and appointed me to the ministry.

—1 Timothy 1:12

But you are a chosen race, a royal priesthood, a holy nation, a people for God's own possession, so that you may declare the goodness of Him who has called you out of darkness into His marvelous light. In times past, you were not a people, but now you are the people of God. You had not received mercy, but now you have received mercy.

—1 Peter 2:9–10

But the anointing which you have received from Him remains in you, and you do not need anyone to teach you. For as the same anointing teaches you concerning all things, and is truth, and is no lie, and just as it has taught you, remain in Him.

—1 John 2:27

ANSWERED PRAYER

Call to Me, and I will answer you, and show you great and mighty things which you do not know.

—Jeremiah 33:3

Ask and it will be given to you; seek and you will find; knock and it will be opened to you.

—MATTHEW 7:7

Therefore I say to you, whatever things you ask when you pray, believe that you will receive them, and you will have them.

—MARK 11:24

If you remain in Me, and My words remain in you, you will ask whatever you desire, and it shall be done for you.

—JOHN 15:7

Confess your faults to one another and pray for one another, that you may be healed. The effective, fervent prayer of a righteous man accomplishes much.

—JAMES 5:16

ANXIETY

Have not I commanded you? Be strong and courageous. Do not be afraid or dismayed, for the LORD your God is with you wherever you go.

—JOSHUA 1:9

The LORD is my shepherd; I shall not want. He makes me lie down in green pastures; He leads me beside still waters. He restores my soul; He leads me in paths of righteousness for His name's sake. Even though I walk through the valley of the shadow of death, I will fear no evil; for You are with me; Your rod and Your staff, they comfort me. You prepare a table before me in the presence of my enemies; You anoint my head with oil; my cup runs over. Surely goodness and mercy shall follow me all the days of my life, and I will dwell in the house of the Lord forever.

—Psalm 23:1–6

My flesh and my heart fails, but God is the strength of my heart and my portion forever.

—Psalm 73:26

Do not be afraid, little flock, for it is your Father's good pleasure to give you the kingdom.

—Luke 12:32

For God has not given us the spirit of fear, but of power, and love, and self-control.

—2 Timothy 1:7

APPEARANCE

But the Lord said to Samuel, "Do not look on his appearance or on the height of his stature, because I have rejected him. For the Lord sees not as man sees. For man looks on the outward appearance, but the Lord looks on the heart."

—1 Samuel 16:7

You brought my inner parts into being; You wove me in my mother's womb. I will praise you, for You made me with fear and wonder; marvelous are Your works, and You know me completely.

—Psalm 139:13–14

Charm is deceitful, and beauty is vain, but a woman who fears the Lord, she shall be praised.

—Proverbs 31:30

In like manner also, that women clothe themselves in modest clothing, with decency and self-control, not with braided hair, gold, pearls, or expensive clothing, but with good works, which is proper for women professing godliness.

—1 Timothy 2:9–10

Do not let your adorning be the outward adorning of braiding the hair, wearing gold, or putting on fine clothing. But let it be the hidden nature of the heart, that which is not corruptible, even the ornament of a gentle and quiet spirit, which is very precious in the sight of God.

—1 Peter 3:3–4

Likewise you younger ones, submit yourselves to the elders. Yes, all of you be submissive one to another and clothe yourselves with humility, because "God resists the proud, but gives grace to the humble."

—1 Peter 5:5

ASSURANCE

He who believes in the Son has eternal life. He who does not believe the Son shall not see life, but the wrath of God remains on him.

—John 3:36

The Spirit Himself bears witness with our spirits that we are the children of God.

—Romans 8:16

For I am persuaded that neither death nor life, neither angels nor principalities nor powers, neither things present nor things to come, neither height nor depth, nor any other created thing, shall be able to separate us from the love of God, which is in Christ Jesus our Lord.

—Romans 8:38–39

Let us draw near with a true heart in full assurance of faith, having our hearts sprinkled to cleanse them from an evil conscience, and our bodies washed with pure water.

—Hebrews 10:22

By this we know that we are of the truth, and shall reassure our hearts before Him. For if our heart condemns us, God is greater than our heart and knows everything. Beloved, if our heart does not condemn us, then we have confidence before God.

—1 John 3:19–21

ATTITUDE

Praise the LORD! Praise God in His sanctuary; praise Him in the firmament of His power! Praise Him for His mighty acts; praise Him according to His excellent greatness! Praise Him with the sound of the trumpet; praise Him with the lyre and harp! Praise Him with the tambourine and dancing; praise Him with stringed instruments and flute! Praise Him with loud cymbals; praise Him with the clanging cymbals! Let everything that has breath praise the LORD. Praise the LORD!

—PSALM 150:1–6

That you put off the former way of life in the old nature, which is corrupt according to the deceitful lusts, and be renewed in the spirit of your mind; and that you put on the new nature, which was created according to God in righteousness and true holiness.

—EPHESIANS 4:22–24

Do all things without murmuring and disputing, that you may be blameless and harmless, sons of God, without fault, in the midst of a crooked and perverse generation, in which you shine as lights in the world.

—PHILIPPIANS 2:14–15

Finally, brothers, whatever things are true, whatever things are honest, whatever things are just, whatever things are pure, whatever things are lovely, whatever things are of good report, if there is any virtue, and if there is any praise, think on these things. Do those things which you have both learned and received, and heard and seen in me, and the God of peace will be with you.

—Philippians 4:8–9

Do not lie one to another, since you have put off the old nature with its deeds, and have embraced the new nature, which is renewed in knowledge after the image of Him who created it.

—Colossians 3:9–10

Humble yourselves in the sight of the Lord, and He will lift you up.

—James 4:10

AUTHORITY

But when the Spirit of truth comes, He will guide you into all truth. For He will not speak on His own authority. But He will speak whatever He hears, and He will tell you things that are to come.

—John 16:13

There is therefore now no condemnation for those who are in Christ Jesus, who walk not according to the flesh, but according to the Spirit. For the law of the Spirit of life in Christ Jesus has set me free from the law of sin and death.

—Romans 8:1–2

But He said to me, "My grace is sufficient for you, for My strength is made perfect in weakness." Therefore most gladly

I will boast in my weaknesses, that the power of Christ may rest upon me.

—2 Corinthians 12:9

That He would give you, according to the riches of His glory, power to be strengthened by His Spirit in the inner man, and that Christ may dwell in your hearts through faith; that you, being rooted and grounded in love, may be able to comprehend with all saints what is the breadth and length and depth and height.

—Ephesians 3:16–18

I am confident of this very thing, that He who began a good work in you will perfect it until the day of Jesus Christ.

—Philippians 1:6

BAD HABITS

He who has a deceitful heart finds no good, and he who has a perverse tongue falls into mischief.

—Proverbs 17:20

Now the works of the flesh are revealed, which are these: adultery, sexual immorality, impurity, lewdness, idolatry, sorcery, hatred, strife, jealousy, rage, selfishness, dissensions, heresies, envy, murders, drunkenness, carousing, and the like. I warn you, as I previously warned you, that those who do such things shall not inherit the kingdom of God.

—Galatians 5:19–21

But avoid profane foolish babblings, for they will increase to more ungodliness.

—2 Timothy 2:16

Therefore submit yourselves to God. Resist the devil, and he will flee from you.

—James 4:7

Live your lives honorably among the Gentiles, so that though they speak against you as evildoers, they shall see your good works and thereby glorify God in the day of visitation.

—1 Peter 2:12

BATTLE FOR YOUR MIND

In all these things we are more than conquerors through Him who loved us.

—Romans 8:37

For the weapons of our warfare are not carnal, but mighty through God to the pulling down of strongholds, casting down imaginations and every high thing that exalts itself against the knowledge of God, bringing every thought into captivity to the obedience of Christ.

—2 Corinthians 10:4–5

Therefore this I say and testify in the Lord, that from now on you walk not as other Gentiles walk, in the vanity of their minds.

—Ephesians 4:17

Be anxious for nothing, but in everything, by prayer and supplication with gratitude, make your requests known to God. And the peace of God, which surpasses all understanding, will protect your hearts and minds through Christ Jesus. Finally, brothers, whatever things are true, whatever things are honest, whatever things are just, whatever things are pure, whatever things are lovely, whatever things are of good report, if there is any virtue, and if there is any praise, think on these things.

—Philippians 4:6–8

He has delivered us from the power of darkness and has transferred us into the kingdom of His dear Son.

—Colossians 1:13

BEAUTY

Give to the Lord the glory of His name; worship the Lord in holy splendor.

—Psalm 29:2

Let the beauty of the Lord our God be upon us, and establish the work of our hands among us; yes, establish the work of our hands.

—Psalm 90:17

Who can find a virtuous woman? For her worth is far above rubies.

—Proverbs 31:10

Strength and honor are her clothing, and she will rejoice in time to come. She opens her mouth with wisdom, and in her tongue is the teaching of kindness.

—PROVERBS 31:25–26

Charm is deceitful, and beauty is vain, but a woman who fears the LORD, she shall be praised.

—PROVERBS 31:30

Finally, brothers, whatever things are true, whatever things are honest, whatever things are just, whatever things are pure, whatever things are lovely, whatever things are of good report, if there is any virtue, and if there is any praise, think on these things.

—PHILIPPIANS 4:8

BITTERNESS

Therefore, if you bring your gift to the altar and there remember that your brother has something against you, leave your gift there before the altar and go on your way. First be reconciled to your brother, and then come and offer your gift.

—MATTHEW 5:23–24

Bless those who persecute you; bless, and do not curse.

—ROMANS 12:14

Repay no one evil for evil. Commend what is honest in the sight of all men.

—ROMANS 12:17

Pursue peace with all men, and the holiness without which no one will see the Lord, watching diligently so that no one falls short of the grace of God, lest any root of bitterness spring up to cause trouble, and many become defiled by it.

—Hebrews 12:14–15

Out of the same mouth proceed blessing and cursing. My brothers, these things ought not to be so.

—James 3:10

BINDING THE ENEMY

Your right hand, O Lord, is glorious in power. Your right hand, O Lord, shatters the enemy. In the greatness of Your excellence, You overthrow those who rise up against You. You send out Your wrath; it consumes them like stubble.

—Exodus 15:6–7

Do not store up for yourselves treasures on earth where moth and rust destroy and where thieves break in and steal. But store up for yourselves treasures in heaven, where neither moth nor rust destroy and where thieves do not break in nor steal, for where your treasure is, there will your heart be also.

—Matthew 6:19–21

Look, I give you authority to trample on serpents and scorpions, and over all the power of the enemy. And nothing shall by any means hurt you.

—Luke 10:19

Finally, my brothers, be strong in the Lord and in the power of His might. Put on the whole armor of God that you may be able to stand against the schemes of the devil.

—Ephesians 6:10–11

Be sober and watchful, because your adversary the devil walks around as a roaring lion, seeking whom he may devour.

—1 Peter 5:8

BLESSINGS

Do not fear, for I am with you; do not be dismayed, for I am your God. I will strengthen you, I will help you, yes, I will uphold you with My righteous right hand.

—Isaiah 41:10

Then Jabez called on the God of Israel, saying, "Oh, that You would indeed bless me and enlarge my territory, that Your hand might be with me, and that You would keep me from evil, that it may not bring me hardship!" So God granted what he asked.

—1 Chronicles 4:10

Arise, O Lord! Confront him, cast him down! Deliver my soul from the wicked by Your sword, from men by Your hand, O Lord, from men of the world whose portion is in this life. You fill their belly with Your treasure; they are satisfied with children, and they leave their abundance to their infants.

—Psalm 17:13–14

The Lord has been mindful of us; He will bless us; He will bless the house of Israel; He will bless the house of Aaron. He will bless those who fear the Lord, both the small and great ones. The Lord shall increase you more and more, you and your children.

—Psalm 115:12–14

Give, and it will be given to you: Good measure, pressed down, shaken together, and running over will men give unto you. For with the measure you use, it will be measured unto you.

—Luke 6:38

BOLDNESS IN CHRIST

The Spirit Himself bears witness with our spirits that we are the children of God, and if children, then heirs: heirs of God and joint-heirs with Christ, if indeed we suffer with Him, that we may also be glorified with Him.

—Romans 8:16–17

Now thanks be to God who always causes us to triumph in Christ and through us reveals the fragrance of His knowledge in every place.

—2 Corinthians 2:14

We have such trust through Christ toward God, not that we are sufficient in ourselves to take credit for anything of ourselves, but our sufficiency is from God.

—2 Corinthians 3:4–5

For God, who commanded the light to shine out of darkness, has shone in our hearts to give the light of the knowledge of the glory of God in the face of Jesus Christ.

—2 CORINTHIANS 4:6

Blessed be the God and Father of our Lord Jesus Christ, who has blessed us with every spiritual blessing in the heavenly places in Christ, just as He chose us in Him before the foundation of the world, to be holy and blameless before Him in love.

—EPHESIANS 1:3–4

BREAKTHROUGH

Surely He shall deliver you from the snare of the hunter and from the deadly pestilence. He shall cover you with His feathers, and under His wings you shall find protection; His faithfulness shall be your shield and wall. You shall not be afraid of the terror by night, nor of the arrow that flies by day.

—PSALM 91:3–5

See, I will do a new thing, now it shall spring forth; shall you not be aware of it? I will even make a way in the wilderness, and rivers in the desert.

—ISAIAH 43:19

No weapon that is formed against you shall prosper, and every tongue that shall rise against you in judgment, you shall condemn. This is the heritage of the servants of the LORD, and their vindication is from Me, says the LORD.

—Isaiah 54:17

Then your light shall break forth as the morning, and your healing shall spring forth quickly, and your righteousness shall go before you; the glory of the LORD shall be your reward.

—Isaiah 58:8

Or else how can one enter a strong man's house and plunder his goods unless he first binds the strong man? And then he will plunder his house.

—Matthew 12:29

You are of God, little children, and have overcome them, because He who is in you is greater than he who is in the world.

—1 John 4:4

BROKENNESS

The LORD is near to the broken-hearted, and saves the contrite of spirit.

—Psalm 34:18

He has put a new song in my mouth, even praise to our God; many will see it, and fear, and will trust in the LORD.

—Psalm 40:3

I will praise the name of God with a song, and will magnify Him with thanksgiving.

—Psalm 69:30

Moreover the light of the moon shall be as the light of the sun, and the light of the sun shall be sevenfold, as the light of seven days, in the day that the Lord binds up the breach of His people and heals the wound from His blow.

—Isaiah 30:26

Those from among you shall rebuild the old waste places; you shall raise up the foundations of many generations; and you shall be called, the Repairer of the Breach, the Restorer of Paths in which to Dwell.

—Isaiah 58:12

BURNOUT

For the Lord loves justice, and does not forsake His saints; they are preserved forever, but the descendants of the wicked will be cut off.

—Psalm 37:28

But those who wait upon the Lord shall renew their strength; they shall mount up with wings as eagles, they shall run and not be weary, and they shall walk and not faint.

—Isaiah 40:31

His master said to him, "Well done, you good and faithful servant. You have been faithful over a few things. I will make you ruler over many things. Enter the joy of your master."

—Matthew 25:23

For He says: "In an acceptable time I have listened to you, and in the day of salvation I have helped you." Look, now is the accepted time; look, now is the day of salvation.

—2 Corinthians 6:2

"God shall wipe away all tears from their eyes. There shall be no more death." Neither shall there be any more sorrow nor crying nor pain, for the former things have passed away.

—Revelation 21:4

CHALLENGES

No man will be able to stand against you all the days of your life. As I was with Moses, I will be with you. I will not abandon you. I will not leave you.

—Joshua 1:5

And even to your old age I am He, and even to your graying years I will carry you; I have done it, and I will bear you; even I will carry, and will deliver you.

—Isaiah 46:4

We are troubled on every side, yet not distressed; we are perplexed, but not in despair; persecuted, but not forsaken; cast down, but not destroyed.

—2 Corinthians 4:8–9

I can do all things because of Christ who strengthens me.

—Philippians 4:13

My brothers, count it all joy when you fall into diverse temptations, knowing that the trying of your faith develops patience. But let patience perfect its work, that you may be perfect and complete, lacking nothing.

—James 1:2–4

CHANGE

Be strong and of a good courage. Fear not, nor be afraid of them, for the Lord your God, it is He who goes with you. He will not fail you, nor forsake you.

—Deuteronomy 31:6

God will hear and afflict them, even He who sits enthroned from of old. Selah. Because they do not change, therefore they do not fear God.

—Psalm 55:19

I urge you therefore, brothers, by the mercies of God, that you present your bodies as a living sacrifice, holy, and acceptable to God, which is your reasonable service of worship. Do not be conformed to this world, but be transformed by the renewing of your mind, that you may prove what is the good and acceptable and perfect will of God.

—ROMANS 12:1–2

Listen, I tell you a mystery: We shall not all sleep, but we shall all be changed.

—1 CORINTHIANS 15:51

Every good gift and every perfect gift is from above and comes down from the Father of lights, with whom is no change or shadow of turning.

—JAMES 1:17

CHARACTER

Blessed is the man who walks not in the counsel of the ungodly, nor stands in the path of sinners, nor sits in the seat of scoffers; but his delight is in the law of the LORD, and in His law he meditates day and night. He will be like a tree planted by the rivers of water, that brings forth its fruit in its season; its leaf will not wither, and whatever he does will prosper.

—PSALM 1:1–3

For to a man who is pleasing before Him, God gives wisdom, knowledge, and joy; but to the sinner He gives the work of gathering and collecting to give him who is pleasing before God. Also this is vanity and chasing the wind.

—ECCLESIASTES 2:26

But the noble devises noble things, and by noble things he stands.

—Isaiah 32:8

Therefore, my beloved, as you have always obeyed, not only in my presence, but so much more in my absence, work out your own salvation with fear and trembling. For God is the One working in you, both to will and to do His good pleasure. Do all things without murmuring and disputing, that you may be blameless and harmless, sons of God, without fault, in the midst of a crooked and perverse generation, in which you shine as lights in the world.

—Philippians 2:12–15

Remembering without ceasing your work of faith, labor of love, and patient hope in our Lord Jesus Christ in the sight of God and our Father.

—1 Thessalonians 1:3

CHARITY

Blessed are those who consider the poor; the Lord will deliver them in the day of trouble. The Lord will preserve them and keep them alive, and they will be blessed on the earth, and You will not deliver them to the will of their enemies.

—Psalm 41:1–2

There is one who scatters, yet increases; and there is one who withholds more than is right, but it leads to poverty. The generous soul will be made rich, and he who waters will be watered also himself.

—Proverbs 11:24–25

Be sure that you not do your charitable deeds before men to be seen by them. Otherwise you have no reward from your Father who is in heaven. Therefore, when you do your charitable deeds, do not sound a trumpet before you as the hypocrites do in the synagogues and in the streets, that they may be honored by men. Truly I say to you, they have their reward. But when you do your charitable deeds, do not let your left hand know what your right hand is doing, that your charitable deeds may be in secret. And your Father who sees in secret will Himself reward you openly.

—Matthew 6:1–4

Give, and it will be given to you: Good measure, pressed down, shaken together, and running over will men give unto you. For with the measure you use, it will be measured unto you.

—Luke 6:38

So now abide faith, hope, and love, these three. But the greatest of these is love.

—1 Corinthians 13:13

CHILDREN

Look, children are gift of the Lord, and the fruit of the womb is a reward. As arrows in the hand of a mighty warrior, so are the children of one's youth. Happy is the man who has his quiver full of them; he shall not be ashamed when he speaks with the enemies at the gate.

—Psalm 127:3–5

Train up a child in the way he should go, and when he is old he will not depart from it.

—Proverbs 22:6

But when Jesus saw it, He was very displeased and said to them, "Allow the little children to come to Me, and do not forbid them, for of such is the kingdom of God. Truly I say to you, whoever does not receive the kingdom of God as a little child shall not enter it." And He took them up in His arms, put His hands on them, and blessed them.

—Mark 10:14–16

For the promise is to you, and to your children, and to all who are far away, as many as the Lord our God will call.

—Acts 2:39

They said, "Believe in the Lord Jesus Christ, and you and your household will be saved."

—Acts 16:31

CHILDREN'S DUTIES

Every one of you shall revere his mother and his father, and you will keep My Sabbaths: I am the Lord your God.

—Leviticus 19:3

Honor your father and your mother, just as the Lord your God has commanded you, that your days may be prolonged, and that it may go well with you in the land which the Lord your God is giving you.

—Deuteronomy 5:16

"Cursed is he who disrespects his father or his mother." And all the people shall say, "Amen."

—Deuteronomy 27:16

Now therefore listen to me, O you children, for blessed are those who keep my ways. Hear instruction, and be wise, and do not refuse it.

—Proverbs 8:32–33

Children, obey your parents in the Lord, for this is right. "Honor your father and mother," which is the first commandment with a promise, "so that it may be well with you and you may live long on the earth."

—Ephesians 6:1–3

CHRISTLIKENESS

For those whom He foreknew, He predestined to be conformed to the image of His Son, so that He might be the firstborn among many brothers.

—Romans 8:29

But we all, seeing the glory of the Lord with unveiled faces, as in a mirror, are being transformed into the same image from glory to glory by the Spirit of the Lord.

—2 Corinthians 3:18

But, speaking the truth in love, we may grow up in all things into Him, who is the head, Christ Himself.

—Ephesians 4:15

Therefore, my beloved, as you have always obeyed, not only in my presence, but so much more in my absence, work out your own salvation with fear and trembling. For God is the One working in you, both to will and to do His good pleasure.

—Philippians 2:12–13

But grow in the grace and knowledge of our Lord and Savior Jesus Christ. To Him be glory, both now and forever. Amen.

—2 Peter 3:18

COMMITMENT

And I will give them one heart and one way, that they may fear Me forever, for their good and for their children after them. And I will make an everlasting covenant with them that I will not turn away from them, to do them good. But I will put My fear in their hearts so that they shall not depart from Me.

—Jeremiah 32:39–40

But let your "Yes" mean "Yes," and "No" mean "No." For whatever is more than these comes from the evil one.

—MATTHEW 5:37

Whoever will confess Me before men, him will I confess also before My Father who is in heaven. But whoever will deny Me before men, him will I also deny before My Father who is in heaven.

—MATTHEW 10:32–33

If a man does not remain in Me, he is thrown out as a branch and withers. And they gather them and throw them into the fire, and they are burned. If you remain in Me, and My words remain in you, you will ask whatever you desire, and it shall be done for you.

—JOHN 15:6–7

For I am persuaded that neither death nor life, neither angels nor principalities nor powers, neither things present nor things to come, neither height nor depth, nor any other created thing, shall be able to separate us from the love of God, which is in Christ Jesus our Lord.

—ROMANS 8:38–39

COMPASSION

Nothing of the cursed thing there must cling to your hand, so that the LORD may turn from the fierceness of His anger and show you mercy, have compassion on you, and multiply you, just as He swore to your fathers.

—Deuteronomy 13:17

A good man shows generous favor, and lends; he will guide his affairs with justice.

—Psalm 112:5

He has given away freely; he has given to the poor; his righteousness endures forever; his horn shall be exalted with honor.

—Psalm 112:9

He who has pity on the poor lends to the Lord, and He will repay what he has given.

—Proverbs 19:17

Thus says the Lord of Hosts: Execute true justice, show mercy and compassion, every man to his brother. Do not oppress the widow, orphan, sojourner, or poor. And let none of you contemplate evil deeds in your hearts against his brother.

—Zechariah 7:9–10

COMPLAINING

Let no unwholesome word proceed out of your mouth, but only that which is good for building up, that it may give grace to the listeners.

—Ephesians 4:29

Do all things without murmuring and disputing.

—Philippians 2:14

In everything give thanks, for this is the will of God in Christ Jesus concerning you.

—1 Thessalonians 5:18

Do not grumble against one another, brothers, lest you be condemned. Look, the Judge is standing at the door.

—James 5:9

Show hospitality to one another without complaining. As everyone has received a gift, even so serve one another with it, as good stewards of the manifold grace of God.

—1 Peter 4:9–10

COMPROMISE

Now fear the Lord, and serve Him with sincerity and faithfulness. Put away the gods your fathers served beyond the River and in Egypt. Serve the Lord. If it is displeasing to you to serve the Lord, then choose today whom you will serve, if it should be the gods your fathers served beyond the River or the gods of the Amorites' land where you are now living. Yet as for me and my house, we will serve the Lord.

—Joshua 24:14–15

He who has no rule over his own spirit is like a city that is broken down and without walls.

—Proverbs 25:28

He answered, "'You shall love the Lord your God with all your heart, and with all your soul, and with all your strength, and with all your mind' and 'your neighbor as yourself.'"

—Luke 10:27

If you love Me, keep My commandments.

—John 14:15

Therefore, to him who knows to do good and does not do it, it is sin.

—James 4:17

CONCEIT

For wisdom is better than rubies, and all the things that may be desired are not to be compared to it. "I, wisdom, dwell with prudence, and find out knowledge and discretion."

—Proverbs 8:11–12

Pride goes before destruction, and a haughty spirit before a fall. Better it is to be of a humble spirit with the lowly than to divide the spoil with the proud.

—Proverbs 16:18–19

See, the Lord, the Lord of Hosts, shall lop the bough with terror; and the tall ones of stature shall be hewn down, and the haughty shall be humbled.

—Isaiah 10:33

Be of the same mind toward one another. Do not be haughty, but associate with the lowly. Do not pretend to be wiser than you are.

—Romans 12:16

Let nothing be done out of strife or conceit, but in humility let each esteem the other better than himself.

—Philippians 2:3

CONDEMNATION

Let the wicked forsake his way, and the unrighteous man his thoughts; and let him return to the Lord, and He will have mercy upon him, and to our God, for He will abundantly pardon.

—Isaiah 55:7

And He said, "What comes out of a man is what defiles a man. For from within, out of the heart of men, proceed evil thoughts, adultery, fornication, murder, theft, covetousness, wickedness, deceit, licentiousness, an evil eye, blasphemy, pride and foolishness. All these evil things come from within and defile a man."

—Mark 7:20–23

For all have sinned and come short of the glory of God.

—Romans 3:23

There is therefore now no condemnation for those who are in Christ Jesus, who walk not according to the flesh, but according to the Spirit. For the law of the Spirit of life in Christ Jesus has set me free from the law of sin and death.

—Romans 8:1–2

Who is he who condemns? It is Christ who died, yes, who is risen, who is also at the right hand of God, who also intercedes for us.

—Romans 8:34

CONFIDENCE

For You are my hope, O Lord God; You are my confidence from my youth.

—Psalm 71:5

In the fear of the Lord is strong confidence, and His children will have a place of refuge.

—Proverbs 14:26

Do not trust in a companion, do not rely on a friend; from her who lies in your embrace, guard the doors of your mouth. For the son dishonors the father, the daughter rises up against her mother, the daughter-in-law against her mother-in-law—the enemies of a man are members of his own household. But as for me, I watch for the Lord; I await the God of my salvation; my God will hear me.

—Micah 7:5–7

I have confidence in you through the Lord that you will not think otherwise.

—Galatians 5:10

Therefore do not throw away your confidence, which will be greatly rewarded.

—Hebrews 10:35

This is the confidence that we have in Him, that if we ask anything according to His will, He hears us. So if we know that He hears whatever we ask, we know that we have whatever we asked of Him.

—1 John 5:14–15

CONFLICT

You shall not take vengeance, nor bear any grudge against the children of your people, but you shall love your neighbor as yourself: I am the Lord.

—Leviticus 19:18

Behold, how good and how pleasant it is for brothers to dwell together in unity!

—Psalm 133:1

Make no friendship with an angry man, and with a furious man you will not go, lest you learn his ways and get a snare to your soul.

—Proverbs 22:24–25

But I say to you, love your enemies, bless those who curse you, do good to those who hate you, and pray for those who spitefully use you and persecute you.

—MATTHEW 5:44

Now may the God of perseverance and encouragement grant you to live in harmony with one another in accordance with Christ Jesus, so that together you may with one voice glorify the God and Father of our Lord Jesus Christ. Therefore welcome one another, just as Christ also welcomed us, for the glory of God.

—ROMANS 15:5–7

CONSEQUENCES

But your iniquities have made a separation between you and your God, and your sins have hidden His face from you so that He will not hear.

—ISAIAH 59:2

The heart is more deceitful than all things and desperately wicked; who can understand it? I, the LORD, search the heart, I test the mind, even to give to every man according to his ways, and according to the fruit of his deeds.

—JEREMIAH 17:9–10

Rulers are not a terror to good works, but to evil works. Do you wish to have no fear of the authority? Do what is good, and you will have praise from him, for he is the servant of God for your good.

—ROMANS 13:3–4

Be not deceived. God is not mocked. For whatever a man sows, that will he also reap. For the one who sows to his own flesh will from the flesh reap corruption, but the one who sows to the Spirit will from the Spirit reap eternal life.

—GALATIANS 6:7–8

For whoever shall keep the whole law and yet offend in one point is guilty of breaking the whole law.

—JAMES 2:10

CONTENTMENT

The LORD is the portion of my inheritance and of my cup; You support my lot. The lines have fallen for me in pleasant places; yes, an inheritance is beautiful for me.

—PSALM 16:5–6

Better is a little that the righteous has than the abundance of many wicked. For the arms of the wicked will be broken, but the LORD supports the righteous.

—PSALM 37:16–17

Better is little with the fear of the LORD than great treasure with trouble. Better is a dinner of herbs where love is than a fatted calf with hatred.

—PROVERBS 15:16–17

I experienced that there is nothing better for them than to be glad and do good in their life. And also that everyone should eat and drink and experience good in all their labor. This is a gift of God.

—Ecclesiastes 3:12–13

I do not speak because I have need, for I have learned in whatever state I am to be content. I know both how to face humble circumstances and how to have abundance. Everywhere and in all things I have learned the secret, both to be full and to be hungry, both to abound and to suffer need. I can do all things because of Christ who strengthens me.

—Philippians 4:11–13

COURAGE

Be strong and of a good courage. Fear not, nor be afraid of them, for the Lord your God, it is He who goes with you. He will not fail you, nor forsake you.

—Deuteronomy 31:6

Have not I commanded you? Be strong and courageous. Do not be afraid or dismayed, for the Lord your God is with you wherever you go.

—Joshua 1:9

I love You, O Lord, my strength. The Lord is my pillar, and my fortress, and my deliverer; my God, my rock, in whom I take refuge; my shield, and the horn of my salvation, my high tower.

—Psalm 18:1–2

Do not fear, for I am with you; do not be dismayed, for I am your God. I will strengthen you, I will help you, yes, I will uphold you with My righteous right hand.

—Isaiah 41:10

When you pass through waters, I will be with you. And through the rivers, they shall not overflow you. When you walk through the fire, you shall not be burned, nor shall the flame kindle on you. For I am the Lord your God, the Holy One of Israel, your Savior; I gave Egypt for your ransom, Ethiopia and Seba in your place. Since you were precious in My sight, you have been honorable, and I have loved you; therefore, I will give men for you, and people for your life.

—Isaiah 43:2–4

CREATIVITY

And He has filled him with the Spirit of God, in wisdom, in understanding, and in knowledge, and in all manner of craftsmanship, to design artistic works, to work in gold, in silver, and in bronze, and in the cutting of stones for settings and in the carving of wood in order to make every manner of artistic work.

—Exodus 35:31–33

She makes herself coverings of tapestry; her clothing is silk and purple....She makes fine linen and sells it, and delivers sashes to the merchant.

—Proverbs 31:22–24

For I would that all men were even as I myself. But every man has his proper gift from God, one after this manner and another after that.

—1 Corinthians 7:7

We have diverse gifts according to the grace that is given to us: if prophecy, according to the proportion of faith; if service, in serving; he who teaches, in teaching; he who exhorts, in exhortation; he who gives, with generosity; he who rules, with diligence; he who shows mercy, with cheerfulness.

—Romans 12:6–8

Every good gift and every perfect gift is from above and comes down from the Father of lights, with whom is no change or shadow of turning.

—James 1:17

CRISIS

The righteous cry out, and the Lord hears, and delivers them out of all their troubles. The Lord is near to the brokenhearted, and saves the contrite of spirit. Many are the afflictions of the righteous, but the Lord delivers him out of them all. A righteous one keeps all his bones; not one of them is broken.

—Psalm 34:17–20

But he who endures to the end shall be saved.

—Matthew 24:13

Therefore watch always and pray that you may be counted worthy to escape all these things that will happen and to stand before the Son of Man.

—Luke 21:36

He said to them, "It is not for you to know the times or the dates, which the Father has fixed by His own authority. But you shall receive power when the Holy Spirit comes upon you. And you shall be My witnesses in Jerusalem, and in all Judea and Samaria, and to the ends of the earth."

—Acts 1:7–8

But He said to me, "My grace is sufficient for you, for My strength is made perfect in weakness." Therefore most gladly I will boast in my weaknesses, that the power of Christ may rest upon me.

—2 Corinthians 12:9

CRITICISM

O Lord my God, in You I put my trust; save me from all those who persecute me, and deliver me.

—Psalm 7:1

When pride comes, then comes shame; but with the humble is wisdom.

—Proverbs 11:2

Blessed are you when men revile you, and persecute you, and say all kinds of evil against you falsely for My sake.

—Matthew 5:11

You have heard that it was said, "You shall love your neighbor and hate your enemy." But I say to you, love your enemies, bless those who curse you, do good to those who hate you, and pray for those who spitefully use you and persecute you.

—Matthew 5:43–44

Remember the word that I said to you: "A servant is not greater than his master." If they persecuted Me, they will also persecute you. If they kept My words, they will keep yours also.

—John 15:20

DECEIT

His grave was assigned with the wicked, yet with the rich in his death, because he had done no violence, nor was any deceit in his mouth.

—Isaiah 53:9

The heart is more deceitful than all things and desperately wicked; who can understand it? I, the Lord, search the heart,

I test the mind, even to give to every man according to his ways, and according to the fruit of his deeds.

—Jeremiah 17:9–10

Let no one deceive you with empty words, for because of these things the wrath of God is coming upon the sons of disobedience.

—Ephesians 5:6

But exhort one another daily, while it is called "Today," lest any of you be hardened through the deceitfulness of sin.

—Hebrews 3:13

For "He who would love life and see good days, let him keep his tongue from evil, and his lips from speaking deceit.

—1 Peter 3:10

DELIVERANCE

He said: The Lord is my rock and my fortress and my deliverer.

—2 Samuel 22:2

For You will cause my lamp to shine; the Lord my God will enlighten my darkness. For by You I can run through a troop, and by my God I can leap a wall.

—Psalm 18:28–29

Many are the afflictions of the righteous, but the Lord delivers him out of them all. A righteous one keeps all his bones; not one of them is broken. Evil will slay the wicked, and those who hate the righteous will be condemned. The Lord redeems the life of His servants, and all who take refuge in Him will not be punished.

—Psalm 34:19–22

But the mercy of the Lord is from everlasting to everlasting upon those who fear Him, and His righteousness to children's children, to those who keep His covenant, and to those who remember to do His commandments.

—Psalm 103:17–18

Awake, awake! Put on your strength, O Zion; put on your beautiful garments, O Jerusalem, the holy city. For the uncircumcised and the unclean will no longer enter you. Shake yourself from the dust; arise, O captive Jerusalem. Loose yourself from the bonds of your neck, O captive daughter of Zion.

—Isaiah 52:1–2

DEPRESSION

The eternal God is your refuge, and underneath you are the everlasting arms; He will drive out the enemy before you, and will say, "Destroy them."

—Deuteronomy 33:27

For You are my lamp, O Lord; the Lord illuminates my darkness.

—2 Samuel 22:29

Then he said to them, "Go your way. Eat the fat, drink the sweet drink, and send portions to those for whom nothing is prepared; for this day is holy to our Lord. Do not be grieved, for the joy of the Lord is your strength."

—Nehemiah 8:10

The steps of a man are made firm by the Lord; He delights in his way. Though he falls, he will not be hurled down, for the Lord supports him with His hand.

—Psalm 37:23–24

Respond to me quickly, O Lord, my spirit fails; do not hide Your face from me, lest I be like those who go down into the pit. Cause me to hear Your lovingkindness in the morning; for in You I have my trust; cause me to know the way I should walk, for I lift up my soul unto You.

—Psalm 143:7–8

DESERTED BY LOVED ONES

If my father and my mother forsake me, then the Lord will take me in.

—Psalm 27:10

He heals the broken in heart, and binds up their wounds.

—Psalm 147:3

I will not leave you fatherless. I will come to you.

—John 14:18

We know that all things work together for good to those who love God, to those who are called according to His purpose.

—Romans 8:28

Cast all your care upon Him, because He cares for you.

—1 Peter 5:7

DIFFERENCES

You shall not take vengeance, nor bear any grudge against the children of your people, but you shall love your neighbor as yourself: I am the Lord.

—Leviticus 19:18

For if you forgive men for their sins, your heavenly Father will also forgive you. But if you do not forgive men for their sins, neither will your Father forgive your sins.

—Matthew 6:14–15

He looked up and saw the rich putting their gifts in the treasury. He also saw a poor widow putting in two mites, and He said, "Truly I tell you, this poor widow has put in more than all of them. For all these out of their abundance have put in their gifts for God. But she out of her poverty has put in all the living she had."

—Luke 21:1–4

I can do nothing of Myself. As I hear, I judge. My judgment is just, because I seek not My own will, but the will of the Father who sent Me.

—John 5:30

Do not be unequally yoked together with unbelievers. For what fellowship has righteousness with unrighteousness? What communion has light with darkness?

—2 Corinthians 6:14

DISAPPOINTMENT

You are my hiding place; You will preserve me from trouble; You will surround me with shouts of deliverance. Selah

—Psalm 32:7

Those who know Your name will put their trust in You, for You, Lord, have not forsaken those who seek You.

—Psalm 9:10

The eye of the Lord is on those who fear Him, on those who hope in His lovingkindness.

—Psalm 33:18

Trust in Him at all times; you people, pour out your heart before Him; God is a shelter for us. Selah

—Psalm 62:8

In the day of prosperity be joyful, but in the day of distress consider: God has made the one as well as the other. For this reason man will not be able to understand anything that comes after him.

—Ecclesiastes 7:14

Blessed are you poor, for yours is the kingdom of God. Blessed are you who hunger now, for you shall be filled. Blessed are you who weep now, for you shall laugh.

—Luke 6:20–21

DISCIPLESHIP

Lord, who will abide in Your tabernacle? Who will dwell in Your holy hill? He who walks uprightly, and does righteousness, and speaks truth in his own heart.

—Psalm 15:1–2

The work of righteousness shall be peace, and the effect of righteousness, quietness and assurance forever.

—Isaiah 32:17

But if a man is righteous and does that which is lawful and right…has walked in My statutes, and has kept My judgments to deal truly, he is righteous and shall surely live, says the Lord God.

—Ezekiel 18:5–9

He has told you, O man, what is good—and what does the Lord require of you, but to do justice and to love kindness, and to walk humbly with your God?

—Micah 6:8

He who loves father or mother more than Me is not worthy of Me. And he who loves son or daughter more than Me is not worthy of Me. And He who does not take his cross and follow after Me is not worthy of Me. He who finds his life will lose it, and he who loses his life for My sake will find it.

—Matthew 10:37–39

DISCOURAGEMENT

See, the Lord your God has set the land before you. Go up and possess it, just as the Lord, the God of your fathers, spoke to you. Do not fear or be discouraged.

—Deuteronomy 1:21

Have not I commanded you? Be strong and courageous. Do not be afraid or dismayed, for the Lord your God is with you wherever you go.

—Joshua 1:9

The sacrifices of God are a broken spirit; a broken and a contrite heart, O God, You will not despise.

—Psalm 51:17

I cried out to God with my voice, even to God with my voice; and He listened to me.

—Psalm 77:1

He heals the broken in heart, and binds up their wounds.

—Psalm 147:3

We are troubled on every side, yet not distressed; we are perplexed, but not in despair; persecuted, but not forsaken; cast down, but not destroyed; and always carrying around in the body the death of the Lord Jesus, that also the life of Jesus might be expressed in our bodies.

—2 Corinthians 4:8–10

DISTRESS

When the poor and needy seek water, and there is none, and their tongues fail for thirst, I, the Lord, will hear them, I, the God of Israel, will not forsake them.

—Isaiah 41:17

He lifted up His eyes on His disciples, and said: "Blessed are you poor, for yours is the kingdom of God. Blessed are you who hunger now, for you shall be filled. Blessed are you who weep now, for you shall laugh."

—Luke 6:20–21

Take heed to yourselves, lest your hearts become burdened by excessiveness and drunkenness and anxieties of life, and that Day comes on you unexpectedly. For as a snare it will come on all those who dwell on the face of the whole earth. Therefore watch always and pray that you may be counted worthy to escape all these things that will happen and to stand before the Son of Man.

—Luke 21:34–36

Do not work for the food which perishes, but for that food which endures to eternal life, which the Son of Man will give you. For God the Father has set His seal on Him.

—John 6:27

Listen, my beloved brothers. Has God not chosen the poor of this world to be rich in faith and heirs of the kingdom which He has promised to those who love Him?

—James 2:5

But rejoice insofar as you share in Christ's sufferings, so that you may rejoice and be glad also in the revelation of His glory.

—1 Peter 4:13

DIVORCE

Therefore a man will leave his father and his mother and be joined to his wife, and they will become one flesh.

—Genesis 2:24

It was said, "Whoever divorces his wife, let him give her a certificate of divorce." But I say to you that whoever divorces his wife, except for marital unfaithfulness, causes her to commit adultery. And whoever marries her who is divorced commits adultery.

—Matthew 5:31–32

He said to them, "Whoever divorces his wife and marries another commits adultery against her. And if a woman divorces her husband and marries another, she commits adultery."

—Mark 10:11–12

Now to the married I command, not I, but the Lord, do not let the wife depart from her husband. But if she departs, let her remain unmarried or be reconciled to her husband. And do not let the husband divorce his wife.

—1 Corinthians 7:10–11

But if the unbeliever departs, let that one depart. A brother or a sister is not bound in such cases. God has called us to peace. For how do you know, O wife, whether you will save your husband? Or how do you know, O husband, whether you will save your wife?

—1 Corinthians 7:15–16

Marriage is to be honored among everyone, and the bed undefiled. But God will judge the sexually immoral and adulterers.

—Hebrews 13:4

DOUBT

I will instruct you and teach you in the way which you will go; I will counsel you with my eye on you.

—Psalm 32:8

Trust in the Lord with all your heart, and lean not on your own understanding; in all your ways acknowledge Him, and

He will direct your paths. Do not be wise in your own eyes; fear the Lord and depart from evil. It will be health to your body, and strength to your bones.

—Proverbs 3:5–8

He replied, "Why are you fearful, O you of little faith?" Then He rose and rebuked the winds and the sea. And there was a great calm.

—Matthew 8:26

Then He said to Thomas, "Put your finger here, and look at My hands. Put your hand here and place it in My side. Do not be faithless, but believing."

—John 20:27

If any of you lacks wisdom, let him ask of God, who gives to all men liberally and without criticism, and it will be given to him. But let him ask in faith, without wavering. For he who wavers is like a wave of the sea, driven and tossed with the wind. Let not that man think that he will receive anything from the Lord.

—James 1:5–7

EGO

We who are strong ought to bear the weaknesses of the weak and not please ourselves. Let each of us please his neighbor for his good, leading to edification.

—Romans 15:1–2

Love suffers long and is kind; love envies not; love flaunts not itself and is not puffed up, does not behave itself improperly, seeks not its own, is not easily provoked, thinks no evil.

—1 Corinthians 13:4–5

Let each of you look not only to your own interests, but also to the interests of others. Let this mind be in you all, which was also in Christ Jesus.

—Philippians 2:4–5

If you fulfill the royal law according to the Scripture, "You shall love your neighbor as yourself," you are doing well.

—James 2:8

Whoever has the world's goods and sees his brother in need, but closes his heart of compassion from him, how can the love of God remain in him? My little children, let us love not in word and speech, but in action and truth.

—1 John 3:17–18

EMOTIONAL NEEDS

Indeed, may he deliver the needy when he cries; the poor also, and him who has no helper.

—Psalm 72:12

I will pray the Father, and He will give you another Counselor, that He may be with you forever: the Spirit of truth, whom the world cannot receive, for it does not see Him, neither does it know Him. But you know Him, for He lives with you, and will be in you. I will not leave you fatherless. I will come to you.

—John 14:16–18

But the Counselor, the Holy Spirit, whom the Father will send in My name, will teach you everything and remind you of all that I told you.

—John 14:26

For whatever was previously written was written for our instruction, so that through perseverance and encouragement of the Scriptures we might have hope.

—Romans 15:4

Nevertheless God, who comforts the downcast, comforted us through the coming of Titus, and not only by his coming, but also by the comfort with which he was comforted in you, when he told us about your sincere desire, your mourning, and your zeal toward me, so that I rejoiced even more.

—2 Corinthians 7:6–7

ENVY

Do not envy the oppressor, and choose none of his ways.

—Proverbs 3:31

Do not let your heart envy sinners, but continue in the fear of the Lord all day long.

—Proverbs 23:17

Wrath is cruel, and anger is outrageous, but who is able to stand before envy?

—Proverbs 27:4

Then He said to them, "Take heed and beware of covetousness. For a man's life does not consist in the abundance of his possessions."

—Luke 12:15

Let your lives be without love of money, and be content with the things you have. For He has said: "I will never leave you, nor forsake you."

—Hebrews 13:5

ETERNAL LIFE

So also is the resurrection of the dead. The body is sown in corruption; it is raised in incorruption. It is sown in dishonor, it is raised in glory. It is sown in weakness, it is raised in power. It is sown a natural body, it is raised a spiritual body. There is a natural body, and there is a spiritual body.

—1 Corinthians 15:42–44

We know that if our earthly house, this tent, were to be destroyed, we have an eternal building of God in the heavens, a house not made with hands.

—2 Corinthians 5:1

But is now revealed by the appearing of our Savior, Jesus Christ, who has abolished death and has brought life and immortality to light through the gospel.

—2 Timothy 1:10

Blessed be the God and Father of our Lord Jesus Christ, who according to His abundant mercy has given us a new birth into a living hope through the resurrection of Jesus Christ from the dead.

—1 Peter 1:3

I have written these things to you who believe in the name of the Son of God, that you may know that you have eternal life, and that you may continue to believe in the name of the Son of God.

—1 John 5:13

EXCUSES

A false witness will not be unpunished, and he who speaks lies will not escape.

—Proverbs 19:5

Not everyone who says to Me, "Lord, Lord," shall enter the kingdom of heaven, but he who does the will of My Father who is in heaven.

—Matthew 7:21

He said to another man, "Follow Me." But he said, "Lord, let me first go and bury my father." Jesus said to him, "Leave the dead to bury their own dead. But you go and preach the kingdom of God." Yet another said, "Lord, I will follow You, but let me first go bid farewell to those at my house." Jesus said to him, "No one who puts his hand to the plow and looks back at things is fit for the kingdom of God."

—Luke 9:59–62

Therefore you are without excuse, O man, whoever you are who judges, for when you judge another, you condemn yourself, for you who judge do the same things.

—Romans 2:1

Follow me as I follow Christ. I praise you, brothers, that you remember me in all things and keep the traditions as I delivered them to you.

—1 Corinthians 11:1–2

EXPECTATIONS

Have not I commanded you? Be strong and courageous. Do not be afraid or dismayed, for the Lord your God is with you wherever you go.

—Joshua 1:9

For surely there is an end, and your expectation will not be cut off.

—Proverbs 23:18

For I know the plans that I have for you, says the LORD, plans for peace and not for evil, to give you a future and a hope.

—JEREMIAH 29:11

Accordingly, it is my earnest expectation and my hope that I shall be ashamed in nothing, but that with all boldness as always, so now also, Christ will be magnified in my body, whether it be by life or by death.

—PHILIPPIANS 1:20

Be anxious for nothing, but in everything, by prayer and supplication with gratitude, make your requests known to God.

—PHILIPPIANS 4:6

FAILURE

I will lift up my eyes to the hills, from where comes my help? My help comes from the LORD, who made heaven and earth.

—PSALM 121:1–2

Though I walk in the midst of trouble, You will preserve me; You stretch forth Your hand against the wrath of my enemies, and Your right hand saves me.

—PSALM 138:7

When you pass through waters, I will be with you. And through the rivers, they shall not overflow you. When you walk through the fire, you shall not be burned, nor shall the flame kindle on you.

—ISAIAH 43:2

It is of the LORD's mercies that we are not consumed; His compassions do not fail. They are new every morning; great is Your faithfulness.

—LAMENTATIONS 3:22–23

The LORD is good, a stronghold in the day of distress; and He knows those who take refuge in Him.

—NAHUM 1:7

FAITH

Then a woman, who was ill with a flow of blood for twelve years, came behind Him and touched the hem of His garment. For she said within herself, "If I may just touch His garment, I shall be healed." But Jesus turned around, and when He saw her, He said, "Daughter, be of good comfort. Your faith has made you well." And the woman was made well instantly.

—MATTHEW 9:20–22

Then He touched their eyes, saying, "According to your faith, let it be done for you."

—MATTHEW 9:29

Jesus answered them, "Have faith in God. For truly I say to you, whoever says to this mountain, 'Be removed and be thrown into the sea,' and does not doubt in his heart, but believes that what he says will come to pass, he will have whatever he says.

—MARK 11:22–23

For in it the righteousness of God is revealed from faith to faith. As it is written, "The just shall live by faith."

—Romans 1:17

So then faith comes by hearing, and hearing by the word of God.

—Romans 10:17

FAMILY

Look, children are gift of the Lord, and the fruit of the womb is a reward.

—Psalm 127:3

In the fear of the Lord is strong confidence, and His children will have a place of refuge. The fear of the Lord is a fountain of life, to depart from the snares of death.

—Proverbs 14:26–27

They brought young children to Him, that He might touch them. But the disciples rebuked those who brought them. But when Jesus saw it, He was very displeased and said to them, "Allow the little children to come to Me, and do not forbid them, for of such is the kingdom of God. Truly I say to you, whoever does not receive the kingdom of God as a little child shall not enter it." And He took them up in His arms, put His hands on them, and blessed them.

—Mark 10:13–16

They said, "Believe in the Lord Jesus Christ, and you and your household will be saved." And they spoke the word of the Lord to him and to all who were in his household. In that hour of the night he took them and washed their wounds. And immediately he and his entire household were baptized. Then he brought them up to his house and set food before them. And he rejoiced with his entire household believing in God.

—Acts 16:31–34

But if any do not care for their own, and especially for those of their own house, they have denied the faith and are worse than unbelievers.

—1 Timothy 5:8

FEAR

Even though I walk through the valley of the shadow of death, I will fear no evil; for You are with me; Your rod and Your staff, they comfort me. You prepare a table before me in the presence of my enemies; You anoint my head with oil; my cup runs over.

—Psalm 23:4–5

Do not be afraid of sudden terror, nor of trouble from the wicked when it comes; for the Lord will be your confidence, and will keep your foot from being caught.

—Proverbs 3:25–26

Do not fear, for I am with you; do not be dismayed, for I am your God. I will strengthen you, I will help you, yes, I will uphold you with My righteous right hand.

—Isaiah 41:10

He said to them, "Why are you so fearful? How is that you have no faith?"

—Mark 4:40

Peace I leave with you. My peace I give to you. Not as the world gives do I give to you. Let not your heart be troubled, neither let it be afraid.

—John 14:27

FINANCIAL TROUBLE

Wealth gained by vanity will be diminished, but he who gathers by labor will increase.

—Proverbs 13:11

Bring all the tithes into the storehouse, that there may be food in My house, and test Me now in this, says the Lord of Hosts, if I will not open for you the windows of heaven and pour out for you a blessing, that there will not be room enough to receive it. I will rebuke the devourer for your sakes, so that it will not destroy the fruit of your ground, and the vines in your field will not fail to bear fruit, says the Lord of Hosts.

—Malachi 3:10–11

But this I say: He who sows sparingly will also reap sparingly, and he who sows bountifully will also reap bountifully. Let every man give according to the purposes in his heart, not grudgingly or out of necessity, for God loves a cheerful giver. God is able to make all grace abound toward you, so that you, always having enough of everything, may abound to every good work.

—2 Corinthians 9:6–8

Let your lives be without love of money, and be content with the things you have. For He has said: "I will never leave you, nor forsake you." So we may boldly say: "The Lord is my helper; I will not fear. What can man do to me?"

—Hebrews 13:5–6

I do not speak because I have need, for I have learned in whatever state I am to be content. I know both how to face humble circumstances and how to have abundance. Everywhere and in all things I have learned the secret, both to be full and to be hungry, both to abound and to suffer need. I can do all things because of Christ who strengthens me.

—Philippians 4:11–13

FINDING GOD IN THE VALLEYS

Even though I walk through the valley of the shadow of death, I will fear no evil; for You are with me; Your rod and Your staff, they comfort me.

—Psalm 23:4

Say to those who are of a fearful heart, "Be strong, fear not. Your God will come with vengeance, even God with a recompense; He will come and save you."

—Isaiah 35:4

Therefore, I will allure her, and bring her into the wilderness, and speak tenderly to her. From there, I will give her vineyards to her, and the Valley of Achor as a door of hope. She will respond there as in the days of her youth, and as in the day when she came up out of the land of Egypt.

—Hosea 2:14–15

Every valley shall be filled and every mountain and hill shall be brought low; and the crooked shall be made straight and the rough ways shall be made smooth.

—Luke 3:5

The invisible things about Him—His eternal power and deity—have been clearly seen since the creation of the world and are understood by the things that are made, so that they are without excuse.

—Romans 1:20

FORGIVENESS

If My people, who are called by My name, will humble themselves and pray, and seek My face and turn from their wicked ways, then I will hear from heaven, and will forgive their sin and will heal their land.

—2 Chronicles 7:14

If your enemy is hungry, give him bread to eat; and if he is thirsty, give him water to drink; for you will heap coals of fire upon his head, and the Lord will reward you.

—Proverbs 25:21–22

Let the wicked forsake his way, and the unrighteous man his thoughts; and let him return to the Lord, and He will have mercy upon him, and to our God, for He will abundantly pardon.

—Isaiah 55:7

I will cleanse them from all their iniquity whereby they have sinned against Me. And I will pardon all their iniquities whereby they have sinned and whereby they have transgressed against Me.

—Jeremiah 33:8

Then Peter came to Him and said, "Lord, how often shall I forgive my brother who sins against me? Up to seven times?" Jesus said to him, "I do not say to you up to seven times, but up to seventy times seven.

—Matthew 18:21–22

FRIENDSHIP

A friend loves at all times, and a brother is born for adversity.
—Proverbs 17:17

A man who has friends must show himself friendly, and there is a friend who sticks closer than a brother.
—Proverbs 18:24

I no longer call you servants, for a servant does not know what his master does. But I have called you friends, for everything that I have heard from My Father have I made known to you.
—John 15:15

Rejoice with those who rejoice, and weep with those who weep.
—Romans 12:15

Bear one another's burdens, and so fulfill the law of Christ.
—Galatians 6:2

FRUSTRATION

Cast your burden on the Lord, and He will sustain you; He will never allow the righteous to be moved.
—Psalm 55:22

Call to Me, and I will answer you, and show you great and mighty things which you do not know.
—Jeremiah 33:3

Let us know, let us press on to know the LORD. His appearance is as sure as the dawn. He will come to us like the rain; like the spring rains He will water the earth.

—HOSEA 6:3

Come to Me, all you who labor and are heavily burdened, and I will give you rest. Take My yoke upon you, and learn from Me. For I am meek and lowly in heart, and you will find rest for your souls.

—MATTHEW 11:28–29

We know that all things work together for good to those who love God, to those who are called according to His purpose.

—ROMANS 8:28

FULFILLMENT

The eyes of all wait upon You, and You give them their food in due season. You open Your hand and satisfy the desire of every living thing.

—PSALM 145:15–16

The LORD is my shepherd; I shall not want. He makes me lie down in green pastures; He leads me beside still waters. He restores my soul; He leads me in paths of righteousness for His name's sake. Even though I walk through the valley of the shadow of death, I will fear no evil; for You are with me; Your rod and Your staff, they comfort me. You prepare a table before me in the presence of my enemies; You anoint my head with oil; my cup runs over. Surely goodness and mercy shall follow me all the days of my life, and I will dwell in the house of the Lord forever.

—Psalm 23:1–6

While we were yet weak, in due time Christ died for the ungodly. Rarely for a righteous man will one die. Yet perhaps for a good man some would even dare to die. But God demonstrates His own love toward us, in that while we were yet sinners, Christ died for us.

—Romans 5:6–8

"This is the covenant that I will make with them after those days, says the Lord: I will put My laws into their hearts, and in their minds I will write them," then He adds, "Their sins and lawless deeds will I remember no more."

—Hebrews 10:16–17

His divine power has given to us all things that pertain to life and godliness through the knowledge of Him who has called us by His own glory and excellence, by which He has given to us exceedingly great and precious promises, so that through these things you might become partakers of the divine nature and escape the corruption that is in the world through lust.

—2 Peter 1:3–4

GENEROSITY

There is one who scatters, yet increases; and there is one who withholds more than is right, but it leads to poverty. The generous soul will be made rich, and he who waters will be watered also himself.

—Proverbs 11:24–25

And whoever gives even a cup of cold water to one of these little ones in the name of a disciple, truly I tell you, he shall in no way lose his reward.

—Matthew 10:42

He looked up and saw the rich putting their gifts in the treasury. He also saw a poor widow putting in two mites, and He said, "Truly I tell you, this poor widow has put in more than all of them. For all these out of their abundance have put in their gifts for God. But she out of her poverty has put in all the living she had."

—Luke 21:1–4

Give, and it will be given to you: Good measure, pressed down, shaken together, and running over will men give unto you. For with the measure you use, it will be measured unto you.

—Luke 6:38

In all things I have shown you how, working like this, you must help the weak, remembering the words of the Lord Jesus, how He said, "It is more blessed to give than to receive."

—Acts 20:35

GIFTS FROM GOD

If you then, being evil, know how to give good gifts to your children, how much more will your heavenly Father give the Holy Spirit to those who ask Him?

—Luke 11:13

Jesus answered her, "If you knew the gift of God, and who it is who is saying to you, 'Give Me a drink,' you would have asked Him, and He would have given you living water."

—John 4:10

Being assembled with them, He commanded them, "Do not depart from Jerusalem, but wait for the promise of the Father, of which you have heard from Me.

—Acts 1:4

Peter said to them, "Repent and be baptized, every one of you, in the name of Jesus Christ for the forgiveness of sins, and you shall receive the gift of the Holy Spirit. For the promise is to you, and to your children, and to all who are far away, as many as the Lord our God will call."

—Acts 2:38–39

We have diverse gifts according to the grace that is given to us: if prophecy, according to the proportion of faith.

—Romans 12:6

GIVING

Honor the Lord with your substance, and with the first fruits of all your increase; so your barns will be filled with plenty, and your presses will burst out with new wine.

—Proverbs 3:9–10

Do not withhold good from those to whom it is due, when it is in the power of your hand to do it.

—Proverbs 3:27

Bring all the tithes into the storehouse, that there may be food in My house, and test Me now in this, says the Lord of Hosts, if I will not open for you the windows of heaven and pour out for you a blessing, that there will not be room enough to receive it. I will rebuke the devourer for your sakes, so that it will not destroy the fruit of your ground, and the vines in your field will not fail to bear fruit, says the Lord of Hosts.

—Malachi 3:10–11

In all things I have shown you how, working like this, you must help the weak, remembering the words of the Lord Jesus, how He said, "It is more blessed to give than to receive."

—Acts 20:35

Let every man give according to the purposes in his heart, not grudgingly or out of necessity, for God loves a cheerful giver.

—2 Corinthians 9:7

GOD HEARS OUR PRAYERS

I will bless the Lord at all times; His praise will continually be in my mouth. My soul will make its boast in the Lord; the humble will hear of it and be glad. Oh, magnify the Lord with me, and let us exalt His name together. I sought the Lord, and He answered me, and delivered me from all my fears.

—Psalm 34:1–4

I called on You, for You will answer me, O God; incline Your ear to me, and hear my speech. Show marvelously Your lovingkindness, O Deliverer of those who seek refuge by Your right hand from those who arise in opposition. Keep me as the apple of Your eye; hide me under the shadow of Your wings, from the wicked who bring ruin to me, from my deadly enemies who surround me.

—Psalm 17:6–9

We know that God does not listen to sinners. But if anyone is a worshipper of God and does His will, He hears him.

—John 9:31

For the eyes of the Lord are on the righteous, and His ears are open to their prayers; but the face of the Lord is against those who do evil.

—1 Peter 3:12

This is the confidence that we have in Him, that if we ask anything according to His will, He hears us. So if we know that He hears whatever we ask, we know that we have whatever we asked of Him.

—1 John 5:14–15

GOD IS ALWAYS WITH YOU

Have not I commanded you? Be strong and courageous. Do not be afraid or dismayed, for the Lord your God is with you wherever you go.

—Joshua 1:9

Is not the Lord your God with you? Has He not given you rest all around? For He has given the inhabitants of the land into my hand, and the land is subdued before the Lord and His people.

—1 Chronicles 22:18

The Lord is my shepherd; I shall not want. He makes me lie down in green pastures; He leads me beside still waters. He restores my soul; He leads me in paths of righteousness for His name's sake. Even though I walk through the valley of the shadow of death, I will fear no evil; for You are with me; Your rod and Your staff, they comfort me.

—Psalm 23:1–4

Do not fear, for I am with you; do not be dismayed, for I am your God. I will strengthen you, I will help you, yes, I will uphold you with My righteous right hand.

—Isaiah 41:10

Let your lives be without love of money, and be content with the things you have. For He has said: "I will never leave you, nor forsake you."

—Hebrews 13:5

GOD'S CARE

Bless the Lord, O my soul, and forget not all His benefits, who forgives all your iniquities, who heals all your diseases, who redeems your life from the pit, who crowns you with lovingkindness and tender mercies, who satisfies your mouth with good things, so that your youth is renewed like the eagle's.

—Psalm 103:2–5

I love the Lord, because He has heard my voice and my supplications.

—Psalm 116:1

O Lord, You have searched me and known me. You know when I sit down and when I get up; You understand my thought from far off. You search my path and my lying down and are aware of all my ways.

—Psalm 139:1–3

He who did not spare His own Son, but delivered Him up for us all, how shall He not with Him also freely give us all things?

—Romans 8:32

But He said to me, "My grace is sufficient for you, for My strength is made perfect in weakness." Therefore most gladly I will boast in my weaknesses, that the power of Christ may rest upon me.

—2 Corinthians 12:9

GOD'S FAITHFULNESS

When you are in distress and all these things come upon you, even in the latter days, if you turn to the Lord your God and shall be obedient to His voice (for the Lord your God is a merciful God), He will not abandon you or destroy you or forget the covenant of your fathers which He swore to them.

—Deuteronomy 4:30–31

He remembers His covenant forever, the word that He commanded, to a thousand generations.

—Psalm 105:8

Indeed, I have spoken it; I will also bring it to pass. I have purposed it; I will also do it.

—Isaiah 46:11

But this I call to mind, and therefore I have hope: It is of the Lord's mercies that we are not consumed; His compassions do not fail. They are new every morning; great is Your faithfulness.

—Lamentations 3:21–23

For all the promises of God in Him are "Yes," and in Him "Amen," to the glory of God through us.

—2 Corinthians 1:20

GOD'S FAVOR

By this I know that You favor me, because my enemy does not triumph over me.

—Psalm 41:11

May God be gracious to us, and bless us, and cause His face to shine on us; Selah....God will bless us, and all the ends of the earth will fear Him.

—Psalm 67:1– 7

Do not let mercy and truth forsake you; bind them around your neck, write them on the tablet of your heart, so you will find favor and good understanding in the sight of God and man.

—Proverbs 3:3–4

In righteousness you shall be established; you shall be far from oppression, for you shall not fear, and from terror, for it shall not come near you.

—Isaiah 54:14

No weapon that is formed against you shall prosper, and every tongue that shall rise against you in judgment, you shall condemn. This is the heritage of the servants of the Lord, and their vindication is from Me, says the Lord.

—Isaiah 54:17

Every good gift and every perfect gift is from above and comes down from the Father of lights, with whom is no change or shadow of turning.

—James 1:17

My little children, I am writing these things to you, so that you do not sin. But if anyone does sin, we have an Advocate with the Father, Jesus Christ the Righteous One. He is the atoning sacrifice for our sins, and not for ours only, but also for the sins of the whole world.

—1 John 2:1–2

You are of God, little children, and have overcome them, because He who is in you is greater than he who is in the world.

—1 John 4:4

For the weapons of our warfare are not carnal, but mighty through God to the pulling down of strongholds.

—2 Corinthians 10:4

GOD'S PRESENCE

When you are in distress and all these things come upon you, even in the latter days, if you turn to the Lord your God and shall be obedient to His voice (for the Lord your God is a merciful God), He will not abandon you or destroy you or forget the covenant of your fathers which He swore to them.

—Deuteronomy 4:30–31

As befits His great name, the Lord will not abandon His people. For it has pleased the Lord to make you His people.

—1 Samuel 12:22

Where shall I go from Your spirit, or where shall I flee from Your presence? If I ascend to heaven, You are there; if I make my bed in Sheol, You are there. If I take the wings of the morning and dwell at the end of the sea, even there Your hand shall guide me, and Your right hand shall take hold of me.

—Psalm 139:7–10

Teaching them to observe all things I have commanded you. And remember, I am with you always, even to the end of the age.

—Matthew 28:20

Remain in Me, as I also remain in you. As the branch cannot bear fruit by itself, unless it remains in the vine, neither can you, unless you remain in Me.

—John 15:4

GOD'S PROTECTION

I will say of the Lord, "He is my refuge and my fortress, my God in whom I trust." Surely He shall deliver you from the snare of the hunter and from the deadly pestilence. He shall cover you with His feathers, and under His wings you shall find protection; His faithfulness shall be your shield and wall.

—Psalm 91:2–4

They shall be Mine, says the Lord of Hosts, on the day when I make up My jewels. And I will spare them as a man spares his son who serves him.

—Malachi 3:17

For truly I say to you, whoever says to this mountain, 'Be removed and be thrown into the sea,' and does not doubt in his heart, but believes that what he says will come to pass, he will have whatever he says. Therefore I say to you, whatever things you ask when you pray, believe that you will receive them, and you will have them.

—Mark 11:23–24

Therefore take up the whole armor of God that you may be able to resist in the evil day, and having done all, to stand.

—Ephesians 6:13

Fight the good fight of faith. Lay hold on eternal life, to which you are called and have professed a good profession before many witnesses.

—1 Timothy 6:12

GOD'S WILL

But seek first the kingdom of God and His righteousness, and all these things shall be given to you. Therefore, take no thought about tomorrow, for tomorrow will take thought about the things of itself. Sufficient to the day is the trouble thereof.

—Matthew 6:33–34

For God is the One working in you, both to will and to do His good pleasure.

—Philippians 2:13

In everything give thanks, for this is the will of God in Christ Jesus concerning you.

—1 Thessalonians 5:18

Come now, you who say, "Today or tomorrow we will go into this city, spend a year there, buy and sell, and make a profit," whereas you do not know what will happen tomorrow. What is your life? It is just a vapor that appears for a little while and then vanishes away. Instead you ought to say, "If the Lord wills, we shall live and do this or that."

—James 4:13–15

For it is the will of God that by doing right you may put to silence the ignorance of foolish men.

—1 Peter 2:15

GOSSIP

You shall not go around as a slanderer among your people, nor shall you stand by while the life of your neighbor is in danger: I am the Lord.

—Leviticus 19:16

Keep your tongue from evil, and your lips from speaking deceit.

—Psalm 34:13

I said, "I will take heed of my ways so that I do not sin with my tongue; I will keep my mouth muzzled while the wicked are before me."

—Psalm 39:1

A talebearer reveals secrets, but he who is of a faithful spirit conceals the matter.

—Proverbs 11:13

The words of a talebearer are as wounds, and they go down into the innermost parts of the body.

—Proverbs 18:8

If anyone among you seems to be religious and does not bridle his tongue, but deceives his own heart, this man's religion is vain.

—James 1:26

GRACE

They refused to obey and were not mindful of Your wonders that You performed among them. But they hardened their necks and in their rebellion appointed a leader to return to their bondage. But You are a God ready to pardon, gracious and merciful, slow to anger and abounding in kindness, and did not forsake them.

—Nehemiah 9:17

The Lord will fulfill His purpose for me; Your mercy, O Lord, endures forever; do not forsake the works of Your hands.

—Psalm 138:8

Surely He scorns the scornful, but He gives favor to the humble.

—Proverbs 3:34

We have all received from His fullness grace upon grace. For the law was given through Moses; grace and truth came through Jesus Christ. No one has seen God at any time. The only Son, who is at the Father's side, has made Him known.

—John 1:16–18

But He said to me, "My grace is sufficient for you, for My strength is made perfect in weakness." Therefore most gladly I will boast in my weaknesses, that the power of Christ may rest upon me.

—2 Corinthians 12:9

GRIEF AND DEATH

Precious in the sight of the Lord is the death of His godly ones.

—Psalm 116:15

This is my comfort in my affliction, for Your word revives me.

—Psalm 119:50

Let not your heart be troubled. You believe in God. Believe also in Me.

—John 14:1

For none of us lives for himself, and no one dies for himself. For if we live, we live for the Lord. And if we die, we die for the Lord. So, whether we live or die, we are the Lord's.

—Romans 14:7–8

Listen, I tell you a mystery: We shall not all sleep, but we shall all be changed. In a moment, in the twinkling of an eye, at the last trumpet, for the trumpet will sound, the dead will be raised incorruptible, and we shall be changed. For this corruptible will put on incorruption, and this mortal will put on immortality. When this corruptible will have put on incorruption, and this mortal will have put on immortality, then the saying that is written shall come to pass: "Death is swallowed up in victory. O death, where is your sting? O grave, where is your victory?"

—1 Corinthians 15:51–55

GUIDANCE

I will instruct you and teach you in the way which you will go; I will counsel you with my eye on you.

—Psalm 32:8

Incline your ear and hear the words of the wise, and apply your heart to my knowledge; for it is a pleasant thing if you keep them within you; they will readily be fitted in your lips. That your trust may be in the Lord, I have made known to you this day, even to you.

—Proverbs 22:17–19

For I know the plans that I have for you, says the Lord, plans for peace and not for evil, to give you a future and a hope.

—Jeremiah 29:11

Jesus answered him, "If a man loves Me, he will keep My word. My Father will love him, and We will come to him, and make Our home with him. He who does not love Me does not keep My words. The word which you hear is not Mine, but the Father's who sent Me.

—John 14:23–24

But when the Spirit of truth comes, He will guide you into all truth. For He will not speak on His own authority. But He will speak whatever He hears, and He will tell you things that are to come.

—John 16:13

GUILT

Because if you return to the Lord, your brothers and children will find compassion before those who have taken them captive, in order to return you to this land. For the Lord your God is gracious and compassionate. He will not turn His face from you if you all return to Him.

—2 Chronicles 30:9

He who covers his sins will not prosper, but whoever confesses and forsakes them will have mercy.

—Proverbs 28:13

Come now, and let us reason together, says the Lord. Though your sins be as scarlet, they shall be as white as snow.

—Isaiah 1:18

Therefore, if any man is in Christ, he is a new creature. Old things have passed away. Look, all things have become new.

—2 Corinthians 5:17

Therefore, brothers, we have confidence to enter the Most Holy Place by the blood of Jesus....Let us draw near with a true heart in full assurance of faith, having our hearts sprinkled to cleanse them from an evil conscience, and our bodies washed with pure water.

—Hebrews 10:19–22

HABITS

Put away from you a deceitful mouth, and put perverse lips far from you. Let your eyes look right on, and let your eyelids look straight before you. Ponder the path of your feet, and let all your ways be established. Do not turn to the right or to the left; remove your foot from evil.

—Proverbs 4:24–27

Do not be conformed to this world, but be transformed by the renewing of your mind, that you may prove what is the good and acceptable and perfect will of God.

—Romans 12:2

"All things are lawful to me," but not all things are helpful. "All things are lawful for me," but I will not be brought under the power of anything.

—1 Corinthians 6:12

No temptation has taken you except what is common to man. God is faithful, and He will not permit you to be tempted above what you can endure, but will with the temptation also make a way to escape, that you may be able to bear it.

—1 Corinthians 10:13

Therefore be imitators of God as beloved children.

—Ephesians 5:1

HEALING

Bless the Lord, O my soul, and all that is within me, bless His holy name....who forgives all your iniquities, who heals all your diseases.

—Psalm 103:1–3

But he was wounded for our transgressions, he was bruised for our iniquities; the chastisement of our peace was upon him, and by his stripes we are healed.

—Isaiah 53:5

For I will restore health to you, and I will heal you of your wounds, says the Lord, because they called you an outcast, saying, "This is Zion whom no man cares for."

—Jeremiah 30:17

Then a woman, who was ill with a flow of blood for twelve years, came behind Him and touched the hem of His garment. For she said within herself, "If I may just touch His garment, I shall be healed."

—Matthew 9:20–21

And when the men of that place recognized Him, they sent word to all the surrounding country and brought to Him all who were sick, and begged Him that they might only touch the hem of His garment. And as many as touched it were made perfectly well.

—Matthew 14:35–36

HEAVEN

And I say to you that many will come from the east and west and will dine with Abraham, Isaac, and Jacob in the kingdom of heaven.

—Matthew 8:11

Jesus said to him, "Truly, I tell you, today you will be with Me in Paradise."

—Luke 23:43

In My Father's house are many dwelling places. If it were not so, I would have told you. I am going to prepare a place for you. And if I go and prepare a place for you, I will come again and receive you to Myself, that where I am, you may be also.

—John 14:2–3

But as it is written, "Eye has not seen, nor ear heard, neither has it entered into the heart of man, the things which God has prepared for those who love Him."

—1 Corinthians 2:9

But they desired a better country, that is, a heavenly one. Therefore God is not ashamed to be called their God, for He has prepared a city for them.

—Hebrews 11:16

HELP IN TROUBLES

The Lord is my pillar, and my fortress, and my deliverer; my God, my rock, in whom I take refuge; my shield, and the horn of my salvation, my high tower.

—Psalm 18:2

For You will cause my lamp to shine; the Lord my God will enlighten my darkness.

—Psalm 18:28

Those who sow in tears shall reap in joy. He who goes forth and weeps, bearing precious seed to sow, shall come home again with rejoicing, bringing his grain sheaves with him.

—Psalm 126:5–6

Though I walk in the midst of trouble, You will preserve me; You stretch forth Your hand against the wrath of my enemies, and Your right hand saves me.

—Psalm 138:7

The Lord opens the eyes of the blind; the Lord raises those who are brought down; the Lord loves the righteous.

—Psalm 146:8

HOLINESS

Consecrate yourselves therefore, and be holy, for I am the Lord your God. You shall keep My statutes, and do them; I am the Lord who sanctifies you.

—Leviticus 20:7–8

Now, Israel, what does the Lord your God require of you, but to fear the Lord your God, to walk in all His ways, and to love Him, and to serve the Lord your God with all your heart and with all your soul.

—Deuteronomy 10:12

You must follow after the Lord your God, fear Him, and keep His commandments, obey His voice, and you must serve Him, and cling to Him.

—Deuteronomy 13:4

Only carefully obey the commandment and the law that Moses the servant of the Lord commanded you: to love the Lord your God, to walk in all His ways, to obey His commandments, to cling to Him, and to serve Him with all your heart and soul.

—Joshua 22:5

I urge you therefore, brothers, by the mercies of God, that you present your bodies as a living sacrifice, holy, and acceptable to God, which is your reasonable service of worship. Do not be conformed to this world, but be transformed by the renewing of your mind, that you may prove what is the good and acceptable and perfect will of God.

—ROMANS 12:1–2

HOLY SPIRIT

Turn at my reproof; surely I will pour out my spirit on you; I will make my words known to you.

—PROVERBS 1:23

As for Me, this is My covenant with them, says the LORD: My Spirit who is upon you, and My words which I have put in your mouth shall not depart out of your mouth, nor out of the mouth of your descendants, nor out of the mouth of your descendants' descendants, says the LORD, from this time forth and forever.

—ISAIAH 59:21

I will put My Spirit within you and cause you to walk in My statutes, and you will keep My judgments and do them.

—EZEKIEL 36:27

I will pray the Father, and He will give you another Counselor, that He may be with you forever: the Spirit of truth, whom the world cannot receive, for it does not see Him, neither does it know Him. But you know Him, for He lives with you, and will be in you.

—JOHN 14:16–17

Likewise, the Spirit helps us in our weaknesses, for we do not know what to pray for as we ought, but the Spirit Himself intercedes for us with groanings too deep for words. He who searches the hearts knows what the mind of the Spirit is, because He intercedes for the saints according to the will of God.

—Romans 8:26–27

HOME

These words, which I am commanding you today, shall be in your heart. You shall teach them diligently to your children and shall talk of them when you sit in your house, and when you walk by the way, and when you lie down, and when you rise up.

—Deuteronomy 6:6–7

If it is displeasing to you to serve the Lord, then choose today whom you will serve, if it should be the gods your fathers served beyond the River or the gods of the Amorites' land where you are now living. Yet as for me and my house, we will serve the Lord.

—Joshua 24:15

I will consider the path that is blameless. When will You come to me? I will walk within my house with a perfect heart.

—Psalm 101:2

Better is a dry morsel with quietness than a house full of sacrifices with strife.

—Proverbs 17:1

Children, obey your parents in the Lord, for this is right. "Honor your father and mother," which is the first commandment with a promise, "so that it may be well with you and you may live long on the earth." Fathers, do not provoke your children to anger, but bring them up in the discipline and instruction of the Lord.

—Ephesians 6:1–4

HONESTY

You shall do no unrighteousness in judgment regarding measures in length, weight, or quantity. You shall have honest balances, honest weights, an honest ephah, and an honest hin: I am the Lord your God, who brought you out of the land of Egypt.

—Leviticus 19:35–36

If you sell anything to your neighbor or buy anything from your neighbor, you shall not oppress one another.

—Leviticus 25:14

You shall not therefore oppress one another, but you shall fear your God. For I am the Lord your God.

—Leviticus 25:17

The LORD will judge the peoples; grant me justice, O LORD, according to my righteousness, and according to my integrity within me.

—PSALM 7:8

He who walks righteously and speaks uprightly, he who rejects unjust gain and shakes his hands from holding bribes, who stops his ears from hearing of bloodshed, and shuts his eyes from seeing evil: He shall dwell on high; his place of defense shall be the impregnable rock; his bread shall be given him, his waters shall be sure.

—ISAIAH 33:15–16

HOPE

Because of the hope which is laid up for you in heaven, of which you have already heard in the word of the truth of the gospel.

—COLOSSIANS 1:5

Remembering without ceasing your work of faith, labor of love, and patient hope in our Lord Jesus Christ in the sight of God and our Father.

—1 THESSALONIANS 1:3

Now may our Lord Jesus Christ Himself, and God our Father, who has loved us and has given us eternal consolation and good hope through grace, comfort your hearts and establish you in every good word and work.

—2 Thessalonians 2:16–17

We have this hope as a sure and steadfast anchor of the soul, which enters the Inner Place behind the veil.

—Hebrews 6:19

Through Him you believe in God who raised Him up from the dead and gave Him glory, so that your faith and hope might be in God.

—1 Peter 1:21

HOSPITALITY

When a foreigner sojourns with you in your land, you shall not do him wrong. The foreigner who dwells with you shall be to you as one born among you, and you shall love him as yourself for you were foreigners in the land of Egypt: I am the Lord your God.

—Leviticus 19:33–34

Is it not to divide your bread with the hungry and bring the poor who are outcasts into your house? When you see the naked, to cover him and not hide yourself from your own flesh? Then your light shall break forth as the morning, and your healing shall spring forth quickly, and your righteousness shall go before you; the glory of the Lord shall be your reward.

—Isaiah 58:7–8

For I was hungry and you gave Me food, I was thirsty and you gave Me drink, I was a stranger and you took Me in. I was naked and you clothed Me, I was sick and you visited Me, I was in prison and you came to Me.

—MATTHEW 25:35–36

Do not forget to entertain strangers, for thereby some have entertained angels unknowingly.

—HEBREWS 13:2

If a brother or sister is naked and lacking daily food, and one of you says to them, "Depart in peace, be warmed and filled," and yet you give them nothing that the body needs, what does it profit?

—JAMES 2:15–16

HUMILITY

The fear of the LORD is the instruction of wisdom, and before honor is humility.

—PROVERBS 15:33

Better it is to be of a humble spirit with the lowly than to divide the spoil with the proud.

—PROVERBS 16:19

For he who exalts himself will be humbled, and he who humbles himself will be exalted.

—MATTHEW 23:12

I tell you, this man went down to his house justified rather than the other. For everyone who exalts himself will be humbled, and he who humbles himself will be exalted.

—Luke 18:14

Let this mind be in you all, which was also in Christ Jesus, who, being in the form of God, did not consider equality with God something to be grasped. But He emptied Himself, taking upon Himself the form of a servant, and was made in the likeness of men. And being found in the form of a man, He humbled Himself and became obedient to death, even death on a cross.

—Philippians 2:5–8

HYPOCRISY

Lord, who will abide in Your tabernacle? Who will dwell in Your holy hill? He who walks uprightly, and does righteousness, and speaks truth in his own heart.

—Psalm 15:1–2

For there is no uprightness in their mouth; destruction is in their midst; their throat is an open tomb; they flatter with their tongue.

—Psalm 5:9

Therefore, the Lord said: Because this people draw near with their mouths and honor Me with their lips, but have removed their hearts far from Me, and their fear toward Me is tradition by the precept of men.

—Isaiah 29:13

Why do you see the speck that is in your brother's eye, but do not see the beam that is in your own eye? How can you say to your brother, "Brother, let me remove the speck that is in your eye," when you yourself do not see the beam that is in your own eye? You hypocrite! First remove the beam from your own eye, and then you will see clearly to remove the speck that is in your brother's eye.

—Luke 6:41–42

They profess that they know God, but in their deeds they deny Him, being abominable, disobedient, and worthless for every good work.

—Titus 1:16

INHERITANCE

The righteous will inherit the land, and dwell on it forever.

—Psalm 37:29

An inheritance may be gained hastily at the beginning, but the end of it will not be blessed.

—Proverbs 20:21

Now, brothers, I commend you to God and to the word of His grace, which is able to build you up and give you an inheritance among all who are sanctified.

—Acts 20:32

And if children, then heirs: heirs of God and joint-heirs with Christ, if indeed we suffer with Him, that we may also be glorified with Him.

—Romans 8:17

That the eyes of your understanding may be enlightened, that you may know what is the hope of His calling and what are the riches of the glory of His inheritance among the saints.

—Ephesians 1:18

JEALOUSY

You shall not covet your neighbor's wife, nor shall you covet your neighbor's house, his field, his male servant, his female servant, his ox, his donkey, or anything that belongs to your neighbor.

—Deuteronomy 5:21

Rest in the Lord, and wait patiently for Him; do not fret because of those who prosper in their way, because of those who make wicked schemes.

—Psalm 37:7

Do not envy the oppressor, and choose none of his ways.

—Proverbs 3:31

Then I saw that all toil and every skillful work come from one man's envy of another. This also is vanity and like chasing the wind.

—ECCLESIASTES 4:4

Then He said to His disciples, "Therefore I say to you, do not be anxious for your life, what you will eat, nor for your body, what you will wear. Life is more than food, and the body is more than clothes.

—LUKE 12:22–23

JESUS CHRIST

The Word became flesh and dwelt among us, and we saw His glory, the glory as the only Son of the Father, full of grace and truth.

—JOHN 1:14

That if you confess with your mouth Jesus is Lord, and believe in your heart that God has raised Him from the dead, you will be saved.

—ROMANS 10:9

But now is Christ risen from the dead and become the first fruits of those who have fallen asleep.

—1 CORINTHIANS 15:20

Therefore God highly exalted Him and gave Him the name which is above every name, that at the name of Jesus every knee should bow, of those in heaven and on earth and under the earth, and every tongue should confess that Jesus Christ is Lord, to the glory of God the Father.

—Philippians 2:9–11

For if we believe that Jesus died and arose again, so God will bring with Him those who sleep in Jesus.

—1 Thessalonians 4:14

JOY AND GLADNESS

Then he said to them, "Go your way. Eat the fat, drink the sweet drink, and send portions to those for whom nothing is prepared; for this day is holy to our Lord. Do not be grieved, for the joy of the Lord is your strength."

—Nehemiah 8:10

He fills your mouth with laughing, and your lips with rejoicing.

—Job 8:21

Make a joyful noise unto the Lord, all the earth! Serve the Lord with gladness; come before His presence with singing.

—Psalm 100:1–2

Blessed are you when men hate you, and when they separate you from their company and insult you, and cast out your name as evil, on account of the Son of Man. Rejoice in that day, and leap for joy, for indeed, your reward is great in heaven. For in like manner their fathers treated the prophets.

—Luke 6:22–23

I have spoken these things to you, that My joy may remain in you, and that your joy may be full.

—John 15:11

JUDGING OTHERS

Judge not, and you shall not be judged. Condemn not, and you will not be condemned. Forgive, and you shall be forgiven.

—Luke 6:37

So when they continued asking Him, He stood up and said to them, "Let him who is without sin among you be the first to throw a stone at her."

—John 8:7

Therefore you are without excuse, O man, whoever you are who judges, for when you judge another, you condemn yourself, for you who judge do the same things. But we know that the judgment of God is according to truth against those who commit such things. Do you think, O man, who judges those who do such things, and who does the same thing, that you will escape the judgment of God?

—Romans 2:1–3

Let no unwholesome word proceed out of your mouth, but only that which is good for building up, that it may give grace to the listeners.

—Ephesians 4:29

Do not speak evil of one another, brothers. He who speaks evil of his brother and judges his brother speaks evil of the law and judges the law. If you judge the law, you are not a doer of the law, but a judge. There is one Lawgiver who is able to save and to destroy. Who are you to judge another?

—James 4:11–12

KINDNESS

Bear one another's burdens, and so fulfill the law of Christ.

—Galatians 6:2

And be kind one to another, tenderhearted, forgiving one another, just as God in Christ also forgave you.

—Ephesians 4:32

So embrace, as the elect of God, holy and beloved, a spirit of mercy, kindness, humbleness of mind, meekness, and longsuffering.

—Colossians 3:12

We also were once foolish, disobedient, deceived, serving various desires and pleasures, living in evil and envy, filled with hatred and hating each other. But when the kindness and the love of God our Savior toward mankind appeared, not by works of righteousness which we have done, but according to His mercy He saved us, through the washing of rebirth and the renewal of the Holy Spirit.

—Titus 3:3–5

Finally, be all of one mind, be loving toward one another, be gracious, and be kind. Do not repay evil for evil, or curse for curse, but on the contrary, bless, knowing that to this you are called, so that you may receive a blessing.

—1 Peter 3:8–9

KNOWLEDGE

The fear of the Lord is the beginning of knowledge, but fools despise wisdom and instruction.

—Proverbs 1:7

When wisdom enters your heart, and knowledge is pleasant to your soul.

—Proverbs 2:10

The heart of the prudent gets knowledge, and the ear of the wise seeks knowledge.

—Proverbs 18:15

The Spirit of the Lord shall rest upon him, the Spirit of wisdom and understanding, the Spirit of counsel and might, the Spirit of knowledge and of the fear of the Lord.

—Isaiah 11:2

My people are destroyed for lack of knowledge. Because you have rejected knowledge, I will reject you from being My priest. And because you have forgotten the law of your God, I will also forget your children. As they increased, so they sinned against Me. I will change their glory into shame.

—Hosea 4:6–7

LAZINESS

Go to the ant, you sluggard! Consider her ways and be wise....How long will you sleep, O sluggard? When will you arise out of your sleep?

—Proverbs 6:6–9

This is what I have seen to be good: It is fitting to eat and drink and find enjoyment in all his labor in which he toils under the sun all the days of his life, which God has given to him; for this is his reward. And also everyone to whom God has given wealth and possessions, and given him power to enjoy them, and to receive his reward and to rejoice in his labor—this is the gift of God.

—Ecclesiastes 5:18–19

The roof beams sink in with slothfulness, and with the idleness of one's hands the house drips.

—Ecclesiastes 10:18

Do not be lazy in diligence, be fervent in spirit, serve the Lord.

—Romans 12:11

Let him who steals steal no more. Instead, let him labor, working with his hands things which are good, that he may have something to share with him who is in need.

—Ephesians 4:28

LIGHT OF THE WORLD

Send out Your light and Your truth. Let them lead me; let them bring me to Your holy hill, and to Your dwelling place.

—Psalm 43:3

The day is Yours, the night also is Yours; You have prepared the light and the sun. You have established all the borders of the earth; You have made summer and winter.

—Psalm 74:16–17

The sun shall no longer be your light by day, nor for brightness shall the moon give light to you; but the Lord shall be an everlasting light to you and your God for your glory.

—Isaiah 60:19

You are the light of the world. A city that is set on a hill cannot be hidden.

—Matthew 5:14

Again, Jesus spoke to them, saying, "I am the light of the world. Whoever follows Me shall not walk in the darkness, but shall have the light of life."

—John 8:12

LISTENING

Incline your ear to wisdom, and apply your heart to understanding.

—Proverbs 2:2

Hear counsel and receive instruction, that you may be wise in your latter days.

—Proverbs 19:20

He who is of God hears God's words. Therefore, you do not hear them, because you are not of God.

—John 8:47

Therefore, my beloved brothers, let every man be swift to hear, slow to speak, and slow to anger.

—James 1:19

He who has an ear, let him hear what the Spirit says to the churches. To him who overcomes I will give permission to eat of the tree of life, which is in the midst of the Paradise of God.

—Revelation 2:7

LONG LIFE

You shall walk in all the ways which the Lord your God has commanded you, so that you may live and that it may be well with you, and that you may prolong your days in the land which you shall possess.

—Deuteronomy 5:33

Wisdom is with the elderly, and understanding comes with long life. "With Him are wisdom and strength; He has counsel and understanding."

—Job 12:12–13

"Lord, make me to know my end, and what is the measure of my days, that I may know how transient I am. Indeed, You have made my days as a handbreadth, and my age is as nothing before You; indeed every man at his best is as a breath." Selah

—Psalm 39:4–5

For by me your days will be multiplied, and the years of your life will be increased.

—Proverbs 9:11

And even to your old age I am He, and even to your graying years I will carry you; I have done it, and I will bear you; even I will carry, and will deliver you.

—Isaiah 46:4

LONELINESS

Remember, I am with you, and I will protect you wherever you go, and I will bring you back to this land. For I will not leave you until I have done what I promised you.

—Genesis 28:15

No man will be able to stand against you all the days of your life. As I was with Moses, I will be with you. I will not abandon you. I will not leave you.

—Joshua 1:5

I will lift up my eyes to the hills, from where comes my help? My help comes from the Lord, who made heaven and earth.

—Psalm 121:1–2

Then you shall call, and the Lord shall answer; you shall cry, and He shall say, Here I am. If you take away the yoke from your midst, the pointing of the finger, and speaking wickedness.

—Isaiah 58:9

I will not leave you fatherless. I will come to you.

—John 14:18

LOVE

I love those who love me, and those who seek me early will find me.

—Proverbs 8:17

Jesus said to him, "'You shall love the Lord your God with all your heart, and with all your soul, and with all your mind.' This is the first and great commandment."

—Matthew 22:37–38

A new commandment I give to you, that you love one another, even as I have loved you, that you also love one another. By this all men will know that you are My disciples, if you have love for one another.

—John 13:34–35

You, brothers, have been called to liberty. Only do not use liberty to give an opportunity to the flesh, but by love serve one another. For the entire law is fulfilled in one word, even in this: "You shall love your neighbor as yourself."

—Galatians 5:13–14

Finally, be all of one mind, be loving toward one another, be gracious, and be kind. Do not repay evil for evil, or curse for curse, but on the contrary, bless, knowing that to this you are called, so that you may receive a blessing.

—1 Peter 3:8–9

LOVING ONE ANOTHER

This is My commandment: that you love one another, as I have loved you. Greater love has no man than this: that a man lay down his life for his friends.

—John 15:12–13

Let love be without hypocrisy. Hate what is evil. Cleave to what is good. Be devoted to one another with brotherly love; prefer one another in honor.

—Romans 12:9–10

Love suffers long and is kind; love envies not; love flaunts not itself and is not puffed up, does not behave itself improperly, seeks not its own, is not easily provoked, thinks no evil; rejoices not in iniquity, but rejoices in the truth; bears all things, believes all things, hopes all things, and endures all things. Love never fails. But if there are prophecies, they shall fail; if there are tongues, they shall cease; and if there is knowledge, it shall vanish.

—1 Corinthians 13:4–8

Walk in love, as Christ loved us and gave Himself for us as a fragrant offering and a sacrifice to God.

—Ephesians 5:2

So embrace, as the elect of God, holy and beloved, a spirit of mercy, kindness, humbleness of mind, meekness, and longsuffering. Bear with one another and forgive one another.

—Colossians 3:12–13

LOVING GOD

I love those who love me, and those who seek me early will find me.

—Proverbs 8:17

He answered, "'You shall love the Lord your God with all your heart, and with all your soul, and with all your strength, and with all your mind' and 'your neighbor as yourself.'"

—Luke 10:27

He who has My commandments and keeps them is the one who loves Me. And he who loves Me will be loved by My Father. And I will love him and will reveal Myself to him."

—John 14:21

But as it is written, "Eye has not seen, nor ear heard, neither has it entered into the heart of man, the things which God has prepared for those who love Him."

—1 Corinthians 2:9

Grace be with all those who love our Lord Jesus Christ in sincerity. Amen.

—Ephesians 6:24

LOYALTY

You shall have no other gods before Me.… You shall not bow down to them or serve them; for I, the Lord your God, am a jealous God, visiting the iniquity of the fathers on the children to the third and fourth generation of them who hate Me.

—Exodus 20:3–5

O Lord, the God of Abraham, Isaac, and Israel, our fathers, keep this forever in the thoughts and intentions of the heart of Your people and direct their heart to You.

—1 Chronicles 29:18

That they might set their hope in God and not forget the works of God, but keep His commandments, and they might not be as their fathers, a stubborn and rebellious generation, a generation that did not set their heart steadfast, and whose spirit was not faithful to God.

—Psalm 78:7–8

A man who has friends must show himself friendly, and there is a friend who sticks closer than a brother.

—Proverbs 18:24

If it be so, our God whom we serve is able to deliver us from the burning fiery furnace, and He will deliver us out of your hand, O king. But even if He does not, be it known to you, O king, that we will not serve your gods, nor worship the golden image which you have set up.

—Daniel 3:17–18

LUST

But put on the Lord Jesus Christ, and make no provision for the flesh to fulfill its lusts.

—Romans 13:14

I say then, walk in the Spirit, and you shall not fulfill the lust of the flesh. For the flesh lusts against the Spirit, and the Spirit against the flesh. These are in opposition to one another, so that you may not do the things that you please.

—Galatians 5:16–17

Those who are Christ's have crucified the flesh with its passions and lusts.

—Galatians 5:24

So flee youthful desires and pursue righteousness, faith, love, and peace, with those who call on the Lord out of a pure heart.

—2 Timothy 2:22

We also were once foolish, disobedient, deceived, serving various desires and pleasures, living in evil and envy, filled with hatred and hating each other. But when the kindness and the love of God our Savior toward mankind appeared, not by works of righteousness which we have done, but according to His mercy He saved us, through the washing of rebirth and the renewal of the Holy Spirit.

—Titus 3:3–5

LYING

A faithful witness will not lie, but a false witness will utter lies.

—Proverbs 14:5

A man who bears false witness against his neighbor is like a club, a sword, and a sharp arrow.

—Proverbs 25:18

Do not lie one to another, since you have put off the old nature with its deeds, and have embraced the new nature, which is renewed in knowledge after the image of Him who created it.

—Colossians 3:9–10

But if you have bitter envying and strife in your hearts, do not boast and do not lie against the truth.

—James 3:14

But the cowardly, the unbelieving, the abominable, the murderers, the sexually immoral, the sorcerers, the idolaters, and all liars shall have their portion in the lake which burns with fire and brimstone. This is the second death.

—Revelation 21:8

MARRIAGE

Then Adam said, "This is now bone of my bones and flesh of my flesh; she will be called Woman, for she was taken out of Man." Therefore a man will leave his father and his mother and be joined to his wife, and they will become one flesh. They were both naked, the man and his wife, and were not ashamed.

—Genesis 2:23–25

Wives, be submissive to your own husbands as unto the Lord. For the husband is the head of the wife, just as Christ is the head and Savior of the church, which is His body.

—Ephesians 5:22–23

Wives, submit yourselves to your own husbands, as it is fitting in the Lord. Husbands, love your wives, and do not be bitter toward them.

—Colossians 3:18–19

But if any do not care for their own, and especially for those of their own house, they have denied the faith and are worse than unbelievers.

—1 Timothy 5:8

That they may teach the young women to love their husbands, to love their children, and to be self-controlled, pure, home-makers, good, obedient to their own husbands, that the word of God may not be dishonored.

—Titus 2:4–5

MATERIALISM

He who loves money will not be satisfied with money; nor he who loves abundance with increase. This also is vanity.

—Ecclesiastes 5:10

Do not store up for yourselves treasures on earth where moth and rust destroy and where thieves break in and steal. But store up for yourselves treasures in heaven, where neither moth nor rust destroy and where thieves do not break in nor steal, for where your treasure is, there will your heart be also.

—Matthew 6:19–21

Then He said to them, "Take heed and beware of covetous-ness. For a man's life does not consist in the abundance of his possessions."

—Luke 12:15

Do not be conformed to this world, but be transformed by the renewing of your mind, that you may prove what is the good and acceptable and perfect will of God.

—Romans 12:2

But those who desire to be rich fall into temptation and a snare and into many foolish and harmful lusts, which drown men in ruin and destruction. For the love of money is the root of all evil. While coveting after money, some have strayed from the faith and pierced themselves through with many sorrows.

—1 Timothy 6:9–10

MEEKNESS

But the meek will inherit the earth, and will delight themselves in the abundance of peace.

—Psalm 37:11

A soft answer turns away wrath, but grievous words stir up anger.

—Proverbs 15:1

But with righteousness he shall judge the poor, and reprove with fairness for the meek of the earth. He shall strike the earth with the rod of his mouth, and with the breath of his lips he shall slay the wicked.

—Isaiah 11:4

The meek also shall increase their joy in the Lord, and the poor among men shall rejoice in the Holy One of Israel.

—Isaiah 29:19

Seek the LORD, all you humble of the land, who carry out His judgment. Seek righteousness, seek humility. Perhaps you will be hidden on the day of the LORD's anger.

—ZEPHANIAH 2:3

MERCY

Then He said, "I will make all My goodness pass before you, and I will proclaim the name of the LORD before you. I will be gracious to whom I will be gracious and will show mercy on whom I will show mercy."

—EXODUS 33:19

But the mercy of the LORD is from everlasting to everlasting upon those who fear Him, and His righteousness to children's children.

—PSALM 103:17

Hear my prayer, O LORD, give ear to my supplications; in Your faithfulness answer me, and in Your righteousness.

—PSALM 143:1

He who covers his sins will not prosper, but whoever confesses and forsakes them will have mercy.

—PROVERBS 28:13

But God, being rich in mercy, because of His great love with which He loved us, even when we were dead in sins, made us alive together with Christ (by grace you have been saved).

—EPHESIANS 2:4–5

MONEY

He who is faithful in what is least is faithful also in much. And he who is dishonest in the least is dishonest also in much. So if you have not been faithful in the unrighteous wealth, who will commit to your trust the true riches?

—LUKE 16:10–11

For the love of money is the root of all evil. While coveting after money, some have strayed from the faith and pierced themselves through with many sorrows.

—1 TIMOTHY 6:10

For we brought nothing into this world, and it is certain that we can carry nothing out.

—1 TIMOTHY 6:7

Let your lives be without love of money, and be content with the things you have. For He has said: "I will never leave you, nor forsake you."

—HEBREWS 13:5

Listen, my beloved brothers. Has God not chosen the poor of this world to be rich in faith and heirs of the kingdom which He has promised to those who love Him?

—JAMES 2:5

MORAL PURITY

Do you not know that the unrighteous will not inherit the kingdom of God? Do not be deceived. Neither the sexually immoral, nor idolaters, nor adulterers, nor male prostitutes, nor homosexuals, nor thieves, nor covetous, nor drunkards, nor revilers, nor extortioners will inherit the kingdom of God. Such were some of you. But you were washed, you were sanctified, and you were justified in the name of the Lord Jesus by the Spirit of our God.

—1 Corinthians 6:9–11

Now the works of the flesh are revealed, which are these: adultery, sexual immorality, impurity, lewdness, idolatry, sorcery, hatred, strife, jealousy, rage, selfishness, dissensions, heresies, envy, murders, drunkenness, carousing, and the like. I warn you, as I previously warned you, that those who do such things shall not inherit the kingdom of God.

—Galatians 5:19–21

Finally, brothers, whatever things are true, whatever things are honest, whatever things are just, whatever things are pure, whatever things are lovely, whatever things are of good report, if there is any virtue, and if there is any praise, think on these things.

—Philippians 4:8

You adulterers and adulteresses, do you not know that the friendship with the world is enmity with God? Whoever therefore will be a friend of the world is the enemy of God.

—James 4:4

But as He who has called you is holy, so be holy in all your conduct, because it is written, "Be holy, for I am holy."

—1 Peter 1:15–16

MOTIVES

Every way of a man is right in his own eyes, but the Lord weighs the hearts.

—Proverbs 21:2

Therefore judge nothing before the appointed time until the Lord comes. He will bring to light the hidden things of darkness and will reveal the purposes of the hearts. Then everyone will have commendation from God.

—1 Corinthians 4:5

For am I now seeking the approval of men or of God? Or am I trying to please men? For if I were still trying to please men, I would not be the servant of Christ.

—Galatians 1:10

Let nothing be done out of strife or conceit, but in humility let each esteem the other better than himself.

—Philippians 2:3

But as we were allowed by God to be entrusted with the gospel, even so we speak, not to please men, but God, who examines our hearts.

—1 Thessalonians 2:4

MY CALLING

Look, I give you authority to trample on serpents and scorpions, and over all the power of the enemy. And nothing shall by any means hurt you.

—Luke 10:19

Truly, truly I say to you, he who believes in Me will do the works that I do also. And he will do greater works than these, because I am going to My Father.

—John 14:12

God is faithful, and by Him you were called to the fellowship of His Son, Jesus Christ our Lord.

—1 Corinthians 1:9

Therefore, my beloved brothers, be steadfast, unmovable, always abounding in the work of the Lord, knowing that your labor in the Lord is not in vain.

—1 Corinthians 15:58

All this is from God, who has reconciled us to Himself through Jesus Christ and has given to us the ministry of reconciliation, that is, that God was in Christ reconciling the world to Himself, not counting their sins against them, and has entrusted to us the message of reconciliation.

—2 Corinthians 5:18–19

For God has not called us to uncleanness, but to holiness.

—1 Thessalonians 4:7

NEED CONFIDENCE

For the Lord will be your confidence, and will keep your foot from being caught.

—Proverbs 3:26

Do not fear, for I am with you; do not be dismayed, for I am your God. I will strengthen you, I will help you, yes, I will uphold you with My righteous right hand.

—Isaiah 41:10

Now may the God of hope fill you with all joy and peace in believing, so that you may abound in hope, through the power of the Holy Spirit.

—Romans 15:13

Not that we are sufficient in ourselves to take credit for anything of ourselves, but our sufficiency is from God.

—2 Corinthians 3:5

So we may boldly say: "The Lord is my helper; I will not fear. What can man do to me?"

—Hebrews 13:6

NEED COURAGE

Be strong and of a good courage. Fear not, nor be afraid of them, for the Lord your God, it is He who goes with you. He will not fail you, nor forsake you.

—Deuteronomy 31:6

Have not I commanded you? Be strong and courageous. Do not be afraid or dismayed, for the Lord your God is with you wherever you go.

—Joshua 1:9

Watch, stand fast in the faith, be bold like men, and be strong.

—1 Corinthians 16:13

Then David said to Solomon his son, "Be strong and courageous, and take action. Do not be afraid nor be dismayed for the Lord God, my God, is with you. He will not leave you nor forsake you, until you have finished all the work of the service of the house of the Lord.

—1 Chronicles 28:20

Do not be frightened by your adversaries. This is a sign to them of their destruction, but of your salvation, and this from God.

—Philippians 1:28

OBEDIENCE

Samuel said, "Does the LORD delight in burnt offerings and sacrifices as much as in obeying the voice of the LORD? Obedience is better than sacrifice, a listening ear than the fat of rams.

—1 SAMUEL 15:22

Blessed are those who keep justice and who do righteousness at all times.

—PSALM 106:3

For whoever does the will of My Father who is in heaven is My brother, and sister, and mother.

—MATTHEW 12:50

Do those things which you have both learned and received, and heard and seen in me, and the God of peace will be with you.

—PHILIPPIANS 4:9

And whatever we ask, we will receive from Him, because we keep His commandments and do the things that are pleasing in His sight.

—1 JOHN 3:22

OPPRESSION

He will judge the world in righteousness; He will give judgment to the peoples in uprightness. The LORD also will be a refuge for the oppressed, a refuge in times of trouble. Those who know Your name will put their trust in You, for You, LORD, have not forsaken those who seek You.

—PSALM 9:8–10

Moreover the prince shall not take of the people's inheritance by oppression to thrust them out of their possession. But he shall give his sons inheritance out of his own possession so that My people not be scattered, every man from his possession.

—EZEKIEL 46:18

If you see in a district the oppression of the poor and the violent perversion of justice and righteousness, do not be astounded at the matter; for the high official is watched over by an even higher official, and there are even higher officials over them.

—ECCLESIASTES 5:8

At that time I will deal with all who oppress you; I will save the lame and gather the outcast; I will give them praise and fame in every land where they have been put to shame.

—ZEPHANIAH 3:19

How God anointed Jesus of Nazareth with the Holy Spirit and with power, who went about doing good and healing all who were oppressed by the devil, for God was with Him.

—ACTS 10:38

OVERWHELMED

The righteous cry out, and the LORD hears, and delivers them out of all their troubles. The LORD is near to the broken-hearted, and saves the contrite of spirit. Many are the afflictions of the righteous, but the LORD delivers him out of them all. A righteous one keeps all his bones; not one of them is broken.

—PSALM 34:17–20

Do not fret because of evildoers, nor be jealous of those who do injustice. For they will quickly wither like the grass, and fade like the green herbs. Trust in the LORD, and do good; dwell in the land, and practice faithfulness. Delight yourself in the LORD, and He will give you the desires of your heart.

—PSALM 37:1–4

But Jesus looked at them and said, "With men this is impossible, but with God all things are possible."

—MATTHEW 19:26

But when the Spirit of truth comes, He will guide you into all truth. For He will not speak on His own authority. But He will speak whatever He hears, and He will tell you things that are to come.

—JOHN 16:13

But my God shall supply your every need according to His riches in glory by Christ Jesus.

—Philippians 4:19

PARENTING

I chose him, and he will instruct his children and his household after him to keep the way of the Lord by doing righteousness and justice, so that the Lord may bring to Abraham what He promised him.

—Genesis 18:19

Every one of you shall revere his mother and his father, and you will keep My Sabbaths: I am the Lord your God.

—Leviticus 19:3

You shall teach them to your children, speaking of them when you sit in your house and when you walk by the way, when you lie down, and when you rise up.

—Deuteronomy 11:19

Train up a child in the way he should go, and when he is old he will not depart from it.

—Proverbs 22:6

Correct your son, and he will give you rest; yes, he will give delight to your soul.

—Proverbs 29:17

PATIENCE

Rest in the Lord, and wait patiently for Him; do not fret because of those who prosper in their way, because of those who make wicked schemes.

—Psalm 37:7

The end of a matter is better than the beginning of it, and the patient in spirit than the haughty in spirit.

—Ecclesiastes 7:8

But he who endures to the end shall be saved.

—Matthew 24:13

Not only so, but we also boast in tribulation, knowing that tribulation produces patience, patience produces character, and character produces hope.

—Romans 5:3–4

Love suffers long and is kind; love envies not; love flaunts not itself and is not puffed up, does not behave itself improperly, seeks not its own, is not easily provoked, thinks no evil.

—1 Corinthians 13:4–5

PEACE

The Lord will give strength to His people; the Lord will bless His people with peace.

—Psalm 29:11

I will hear what God the Lord will speak, for He will speak peace to His people and to His saints, but let them not turn again to folly.

—Psalm 85:8

He shall enter into peace; they shall rest in their beds, each one walking in his uprightness.

—Isaiah 57:2

He said, "O man, greatly beloved, do not fear. Peace be unto you. Be strong and courageous!" When he spoke to me, I was strengthened and said, "Let my lord speak, for you have strengthened me."

—Daniel 10:19

Salt is good. But if the salt loses its saltiness, how will you season it? Have salt in yourselves, and have peace with one another.

—Mark 9:50

PERSECUTION

Blessed are those who are persecuted for righteousness' sake, for theirs is the kingdom of heaven. Blessed are you when men revile you, and persecute you, and say all kinds of evil against you falsely for My sake. Rejoice and be very glad, because great is your reward in heaven, for in this manner they persecuted the prophets who were before you.

—Matthew 5:10–12

You will be hated by all men for My name's sake. But he who endures to the end will be saved.

—Matthew 10:22

Remember the word that I said to you: "A servant is not greater than his master." If they persecuted Me, they will also persecute you. If they kept My words, they will keep yours also.

—John 15:20

Bless those who persecute you; bless, and do not curse.

—Romans 12:14

We labor, working with our own hands. Being reviled, we bless. Being persecuted, we endure. Being slandered, we encourage. We are made as the filth of the world, and are the refuse of all things to this day.

—1 Corinthians 4:12–13

PERSEVERANCE

And call on Me in the day of trouble; I will deliver you, and you will glorify Me.

—Psalm 50:15

When you pass through waters, I will be with you. And through the rivers, they shall not overflow you. When you walk through the fire, you shall not be burned, nor shall the flame kindle on you.

—Isaiah 43:2

In your endurance you will gain your souls.

—Luke 21:19

Not only so, but we also boast in tribulation, knowing that tribulation produces patience, patience produces character, and character produces hope. And hope does not disappoint, because the love of God is shed abroad in our hearts by the Holy Spirit who has been given to us.

—Romans 5:3–5

Our light affliction, which lasts but for a moment, works for us a far more exceeding and eternal weight of glory.

—2 Corinthians 4:17

PERSPECTIVE

But the Lord said to Samuel, "Do not look on his appearance or on the height of his stature, because I have rejected him. For the Lord sees not as man sees. For man looks on the outward appearance, but the Lord looks on the heart."

—1 Samuel 16:7

Have you not known? Have you not heard, that the everlasting God, the Lord, the Creator of the ends of the earth, does not faint, nor is He weary? His understanding is inscrutable. He gives power to the faint, and to those who have no might He increases strength.

—Isaiah 40:28–29

For My thoughts are not your thoughts, nor are your ways My ways, says the Lord. For as the heavens are higher than the earth, so are My ways higher than your ways, and My thoughts than your thoughts.

—Isaiah 55:8–9

Teaching them to observe all things I have commanded you. And remember, I am with you always, even to the end of the age.

—Matthew 28:20

If you then, being evil, know how to give good gifts to your children, how much more will your Father who is in heaven give good things to those who ask Him!

—Matthew 7:11

POSITION IN GOD

I am the true vine, and My Father is the vinedresser....I am the vine, you are the branches. He who remains in Me, and I in him, bears much fruit. For without Me you can do nothing.

—John 15:1–5

Do you not know that you are the temple of God, and that the Spirit of God dwells in you?

—1 Corinthians 3:16

But now in Christ Jesus you who were formerly far away have been brought near by the blood of Christ.

—Ephesians 2:13

You are all the sons of light and the sons of the day. We are not of the night nor of darkness.

—1 Thessalonians 5:5

For we have become partakers of Christ if we hold the beginning of our confidence firmly to the end.

—Hebrews 3:14

POVERTY

For the Lord hears the poor, and does not despise His prisoners.

—Psalm 69:33

Indeed, may he deliver the needy when he cries; the poor also, and him who has no helper. May he have compassion on the poor and needy, and save the lives of the needy.

—Psalm 72:12–13

He will regard the prayer of the destitute and will not despise their prayer.

—Psalm 102:17

I will abundantly bless her provisions; I will satisfy her poor with bread.

—Psalm 132:15

Sing to the Lord, praise the Lord. For He has delivered the soul of the poor from the hand of evildoers.

—Jeremiah 20:13

POWER

Yours, O LORD, is the greatness, and the power, and the glory, and the victory, and the majesty, for everything in the heavens and the earth is Yours. Yours is the kingdom, O LORD, and You exalt Yourself as head above all.

—1 CHRONICLES 29:11

The LORD is slow to anger and great in power, and the LORD will in no way acquit the guilty. In gale winds and a storm is His way, and clouds are the dust of His feet.

—NAHUM 1:3

And he said to me: "This is the word of the LORD to Zerubbabel, saying: Not by might nor by power, but by My Spirit, says the LORD of Hosts.

—ZECHARIAH 4:6

But Jesus looked at them and said, "With men this is impossible, but with God all things are possible."

—MATTHEW 19:26

Strengthened with all might according to His glorious power, enduring everything with perseverance and patience joyfully.

—COLOSSIANS 1:11

POWER OF GOD'S WORD

My son, attend to my words; incline your ear to my sayings. Do not let them depart from your eyes; keep them in the midst of your heart; for they are life to those who find them, and health to all their body.

—Proverbs 4:20–22

Every word of God is pure; He is a shield to those who put their trust in Him.

—Proverbs 30:5

Heaven and earth will pass away, but My words will never pass away.

—Matthew 24:35

Sanctify them by Your truth. Your word is truth.

—John 17:17

So then faith comes by hearing, and hearing by the word of God.

—Romans 10:17

For the word of God is alive, and active, and sharper than any two-edged sword, piercing even to the division of soul and spirit, of joints and marrow, and able to judge the thoughts and intents of the heart.

—Hebrews 4:12

POWER OF JESUS' NAME

Then Jesus came and spoke to them, saying, "All authority has been given to Me in heaven and on earth.

—Matthew 28:18

Look, I give you authority to trample on serpents and scorpions, and over all the power of the enemy. And nothing shall by any means hurt you.

—Luke 10:19

On that day you will ask Me nothing. Truly, truly I say to you, whatever you ask the Father in My name, He will give it to you.

—John 16:23

Then Peter said, "I have no silver and gold, but I give you what I have. In the name of Jesus Christ of Nazareth, rise up and walk."

—Acts 3:6

Now, Lord, look on their threats and grant that Your servants may speak Your word with great boldness, by stretching out Your hand to heal and that signs and wonders may be performed in the name of Your holy Son Jesus.

—Acts 4:29–30

POWER OF PRAISE

You alone are the Lord. You have made heaven, the heaven of heavens, with all their host, the earth and all that is on it, the seas and all that is in them; and You preserve them all. And the host of heaven worships You.

—Nehemiah 9:6

Whoever sacrifices a thank offering glorifies Me and makes a way; I will show him the salvation of God.

—Psalm 50:23

O come, let us worship and bow down; let us kneel before the Lord, our Maker. For He is our God, and we are the people of His pasture and the sheep of His hand.

—Psalm 95:6–7

Shout joyfully to God, all you lands! Sing out the glory of His name; make His praise glorious. Say to God, "How awesome are Your works! Through the greatness of Your power Your enemies cringe before You. All the earth will worship You and will sing to You; they will sing to Your name." Selah

—Psalm 66:1–4

I will greatly praise the Lord with my mouth; indeed, I will praise Him among the multitude. For He stands at the right hand of the poor, to save him from those who condemn his soul to death.

—Psalm 109:30–31

Through Him, then, let us continually offer to God the sacrifice of praise, which is the fruit of our lips, giving thanks to His name.

—Hebrews 13:15

POWER OF THE TONGUE

A soft answer turns away wrath, but grievous words stir up anger.

—Proverbs 15:1

Death and life are in the power of the tongue, and those who love it will eat its fruit.

—Proverbs 18:21

Let no unwholesome word proceed out of your mouth, but only that which is good for building up, that it may give grace to the listeners.

—Ephesians 4:29

If anyone among you seems to be religious and does not bridle his tongue, but deceives his own heart, this man's religion is vain.

—James 1:26

For "He who would love life and see good days, let him keep his tongue from evil, and his lips from speaking deceit.

—1 Peter 3:10

PRAYER

He shall call upon Me, and I will answer him; I will be with him in trouble, and I will deliver him and honor him.

—Psalm 91:15

The Lord is far from the wicked, but He hears the prayer of the righteous.

—Proverbs 15:29

Then you shall call, and the Lord shall answer; you shall cry, and He shall say, Here I am. If you take away the yoke from your midst, the pointing of the finger, and speaking wickedness.

—Isaiah 58:9

Call to Me, and I will answer you, and show you great and mighty things which you do not know.

—Jeremiah 33:3

Again I say to you, that if two of you agree on earth about anything they ask, it will be done for them by My Father who is in heaven. For where two or three are assembled in My name, there I am in their midst.

—Matthew 18:19–20

PRAYING WITH POWER

Ask and it will be given to you; seek and you will find; knock and it will be opened to you. For everyone who asks receives, and he who seeks finds, and to him who knocks, it will be opened. "What man is there among you who, if his son asks for bread, will give him a stone? Or if he asks for a fish, will he give him a snake? If you then, being evil, know how to give good gifts to your children, how much more will your Father who is in heaven give good things to those who ask Him!

—Matthew 7:7–11

Likewise, the Spirit helps us in our weaknesses, for we do not know what to pray for as we ought, but the Spirit Himself intercedes for us with groanings too deep for words.

—Romans 8:26

You ask, and do not receive, because you ask amiss, that you may spend it on your passions.

—James 4:3

And the prayer of faith will save the sick, and the Lord will raise him up. And if he has committed any sins, he will be forgiven.

—James 5:15

And whatever we ask, we will receive from Him, because we keep His commandments and do the things that are pleasing in His sight.

—1 John 3:22

PROSPERITY

For you shall eat the fruit of the labor of your hands; you will be happy, and it shall be well with you.

—Psalm 128:2

The blessing of the Lord makes rich, and He adds no sorrow with it.

—Proverbs 10:22

He who is of a proud heart stirs up strife, but he who puts his trust in the Lord will prosper.

—Proverbs 28:25

Bring all the tithes into the storehouse, that there may be food in My house, and test Me now in this, says the Lord of Hosts, if I will not open for you the windows of heaven and pour out for you a blessing, that there will not be room enough to receive it.

—Malachi 3:10

God is able to make all grace abound toward you, so that you, always having enough of everything, may abound to every good work.

—2 Corinthians 9:8

PROTECTION

Of Benjamin he said, "The beloved of the Lord will dwell in safety by Him, and the Lord will protect him all day long. He will dwell between His shoulders."

—Deuteronomy 33:12

The Lord is my light and my salvation; whom will I fear? The Lord is the strength of my life; of whom will I be afraid?

—Psalm 27:1

Because you have made the Lord, who is my refuge, even the Most High, your dwelling, there shall be no evil befall you, neither shall any plague come near your tent.

—Psalm 91:9–10

When you lie down, you will not be afraid; yes, you will lie down and your sleep will be sweet.

—Proverbs 3:24

But now, thus says the Lord who created you, O Jacob, and He who formed you, O Israel: Do not fear, for I have redeemed you; I have called you by your name; you are Mine. When you pass through waters, I will be with you. And through the rivers, they shall not overflow you. When you walk through the fire, you shall not be burned, nor shall the flame kindle on you.

—Isaiah 43:1–2

PROVISION

Now it will be, if you will diligently obey the voice of the Lord your God, being careful to do all His commandments which I am commanding you today, then the Lord your God will set you high above all the nations of the earth. And all these blessings will come on you and overtake you if you listen to the voice of the Lord your God.

—Deuteronomy 28:1–2

I have been young, and now am old; yet I have not seen the righteous forsaken, nor their offspring begging bread. The righteous are gracious and lend, and their offspring are a source of blessing.

—PSALM 37:25–26

God is able to make all grace abound toward you, so that you, always having enough of everything, may abound to every good work.

—2 CORINTHIANS 9:8

I do not speak because I have need, for I have learned in whatever state I am to be content. I know both how to face humble circumstances and how to have abundance. Everywhere and in all things I have learned the secret, both to be full and to be hungry, both to abound and to suffer need.

—PHILIPPIANS 4:11–12

But my God shall supply your every need according to His riches in glory by Christ Jesus.

—PHILIPPIANS 4:19

PUNISHMENT

My son, do not despise the chastening of the LORD, nor be weary of His correction; for whom the LORD loves He corrects, even as a father the son in whom he delights.

—PROVERBS 3:11–12

Your own wickedness will correct you, and your backslidings will reprove you. Know therefore and see that it is an evil thing and bitter for you to have forsaken the Lord your God, and the fear of Me is not in you, says the Lord God of Hosts.

—Jeremiah 2:19

But he who does wrong will receive for the wrong which he has done, and there is no partiality.

—Colossians 3:25

And to give you who are troubled rest with us when the Lord Jesus is revealed from heaven with His mighty angels, in flaming fire taking vengeance on those who do not know God and do not obey the gospel of our Lord Jesus Christ.

—2 Thessalonians 1:7–8

For if the word spoken by angels was true, and every sin and disobedience received a just recompense, how shall we escape if we neglect such a great salvation, which was first declared by the Lord, and was confirmed to us by those who heard Him?

—Hebrews 2:2–3

PURPOSE

The Lord will fulfill His purpose for me; Your mercy, O Lord, endures forever; do not forsake the works of Your hands.

—Psalm 138:8

For I know the plans that I have for you, says the Lord, plans for peace and not for evil, to give you a future and a hope.

—Jeremiah 29:11

We know that all things work together for good to those who love God, to those who are called according to His purpose.

—Romans 8:28

Just as He chose us in Him before the foundation of the world, to be holy and blameless before Him in love; He predestined us to adoption as sons to Himself through Jesus Christ according to the good pleasure of His will.

—Ephesians 1:4–5

For we are His workmanship, created in Christ Jesus for good works, which God prepared beforehand, so that we should walk in them.

—Ephesians 2:10

But you are a chosen race, a royal priesthood, a holy nation, a people for God's own possession, so that you may declare the goodness of Him who has called you out of darkness into His marvelous light.

—1 Peter 2:9

RECONCILIATION

Therefore, if you bring your gift to the altar and there remember that your brother has something against you, leave your gift there before the altar and go on your way. First be reconciled to your brother, and then come and offer your gift. Reconcile with your adversary quickly, while you are on the way with him, lest your adversary deliver you to the judge, and the judge deliver you to the officer, and you be thrown into prison. Truly I say to you, you will by no means come out of there until you have paid the last penny.

—Matthew 5:23–26

For if while we were enemies, we were reconciled to God by the death of His Son, how much more, being reconciled, shall we be saved by His life.

—Romans 5:10

All this is from God, who has reconciled us to Himself through Jesus Christ and has given to us the ministry of reconciliation.

—2 Corinthians 5:18

And be kind one to another, tenderhearted, forgiving one another, just as God in Christ also forgave you.

—Ephesians 4:32

Pursue peace with all men, and the holiness without which no one will see the Lord

—Hebrews 12:14

REDEMPTION

But he was wounded for our transgressions, he was bruised for our iniquities; the chastisement of our peace was upon him, and by his stripes we are healed. All of us like sheep have gone astray; each of us has turned to his own way, but the Lord has laid on him the iniquity of us all.

—Isaiah 53:5–6

The next day John saw Jesus coming toward him and said, "Look, the Lamb of God, who takes away the sin of the world."

—John 1:29

Therefore, brothers, let it be known to you that through this Man forgiveness of sins is proclaimed to you.

—Acts 13:38

Who gave Himself for our sins, that He might deliver us from this present evil age, according to the will of our God and Father.

—Galatians 1:4

This is a faithful saying and worthy of all acceptance, that Christ Jesus came into the world to save sinners, of whom I am the worst.

—1 Timothy 1:15

REJECTION

If my father and my mother forsake me, then the Lord will take me in.

—Psalm 27:10

The righteous cry out, and the Lord hears, and delivers them out of all their troubles. The Lord is near to the brokenhearted, and saves the contrite of spirit. Many are the afflictions of the righteous, but the Lord delivers him out of them all. A righteous one keeps all his bones; not one of them is broken.

—Psalm 34:17–20

For the Lord will not forsake His people; neither will He abandon His inheritance.

—Psalm 94:14

If the world hates you, you know that it hated Me before it hated you.

—John 15:18

Cast all your care upon Him, because He cares for you.

—1 Peter 5:7

RELATIONSHIPS

He who walks with wise men will be wise, but a companion of fools will be destroyed.

—Proverbs 13:20

Two are better than one, because there is a good reward for their labor together. For if they fall, then one will help up his companion. But woe to him who is alone when he falls and has no one to help him up....And if someone might overpower another by himself, two together can withstand him. A three-fold cord is not quickly broken.

—Ecclesiastes 4:9–12

Jesus said to him, "You shall love the Lord your God with all your heart, and with all your soul, and with all your mind." This is the first and great commandment. And the second is like it: "You shall love your neighbor as yourself."

—Matthew 22:37–39

Do not be unequally yoked together with unbelievers. For what fellowship has righteousness with unrighteousness? What communion has light with darkness?…Therefore, "Come out from among them and be separate, says the Lord. Do not touch what is unclean, and I will receive you. I will be a Father to you, and you shall be My sons and daughters," says the Lord Almighty.

—2 Corinthians 6:14–18

With all humility, meekness, and patience, bearing with one another in love, be eager to keep the unity of the Spirit in the bond of peace.

—Ephesians 4:2–3

RENEWAL

Create in me a clean heart, O God, and renew a right spirit within me.

—Psalm 51:10

Do not be conformed to this world, but be transformed by the renewing of your mind, that you may prove what is the good and acceptable and perfect will of God.

—Romans 12:2

No temptation has taken you except what is common to man. God is faithful, and He will not permit you to be tempted above what you can endure, but will with the temptation also make a way to escape, that you may be able to bear it.

—1 Corinthians 10:13

Therefore, if any man is in Christ, he is a new creature. Old things have passed away. Look, all things have become new.

—2 Corinthians 5:17

And have embraced the new nature, which is renewed in knowledge after the image of Him who created it, where there is neither Greek nor Jew, circumcision nor uncircumcision, barbarian, Scythian, slave nor free, but Christ is all and in all. So embrace, as the elect of God, holy and beloved, a spirit of mercy, kindness, humbleness of mind, meekness, and longsuffering.

—Colossians 3:10–12

REPENTANCE

The Lord is near to the broken-hearted, and saves the contrite of spirit.

—Psalm 34:18

But if the wicked turns from all his sins that he has committed, and keeps all My statutes, and does that which is lawful and right, he shall surely live. He shall not die. All his transgressions that he has committed, they shall not be remembered against him. Because of his righteousness that he has done, he shall live.

—Ezekiel 18:21–22

But go and learn what this means, 'I desire mercy, and not sacrifice.' For I have not come to call the righteous, but sinners, to repentance."

—Matthew 9:13

Draw near to God, and He will draw near to you. Cleanse your hands, you sinners, and purify your hearts, you double-minded. Grieve and mourn and weep. Let your laughter be turned to mourning, and your joy to dejection. Humble yourselves in the sight of the Lord, and He will lift you up.

—James 4:8–10

Remember therefore from where you have fallen. Repent, and do the works you did at first, or else I will come to you quickly and remove your candlestick from its place, unless you repent.

—Revelation 2:5

RESPECT

Honor your father and your mother, that your days may be long in the land which the LORD your God is giving you.

—Exodus 20:12

Therefore the LORD God of Israel says, "I surely said that your house, and the house of your father, should walk before Me forever," but now the LORD says, "Far be it from Me to do so, for those who honor Me, I will honor, and those that despise Me will be humbled."

—1 Samuel 2:30

That all men should honor the Son, just as they honor the Father. He who does not honor the Son does not honor the Father who sent Him.

—John 5:23

However, let each one of you love his wife as himself, and let the wife see that she respects her husband.

—Ephesians 5:33

Honor all people. Love the brotherhood. Fear God. Honor the king.

—1 Peter 2:17

REST

It is in vain for you to rise up early, to stay up late, and to eat the bread of hard toil, for He gives sleep to His beloved.

—Psalm 127:2

For thus says the Lord God, the Holy One of Israel: In returning and rest you shall be saved; in quietness and in confidence shall be your strength.

—Isaiah 30:15

He gives power to the faint, and to those who have no might He increases strength. Even the youths shall faint and be weary, and the young men shall utterly fall, but those who wait upon the Lord shall renew their strength; they shall mount up with wings as eagles, they shall run and not be weary, and they shall walk and not faint.

—Isaiah 40:29–31

Do not fear, for I am with you; do not be dismayed, for I am your God. I will strengthen you, I will help you, yes, I will uphold you with My righteous right hand.

—Isaiah 41:10

Come to Me, all you who labor and are heavily burdened, and I will give you rest. Take My yoke upon you, and learn from Me. For I am meek and lowly in heart, and you will find rest for your souls. For My yoke is easy, and My burden is light.

—Matthew 11:28–30

RESTITUTION

When a person sins and acts unfaithfully against the LORD by lying to another concerning something left in storage, or entrusted to him, or theft, or by extorting his neighbor…or about which he swore falsely, then he shall repay it in full and shall add one fifth to it. He shall give it to whom it belongs on the day that he is found guilty.

—LEVITICUS 6:2–5

Men do not despise a thief if he steals to satisfy himself when he is hungry. But if he is found, he will restore sevenfold; he will give all the substance of his house.

—PROVERBS 6:30–31

Whoever, therefore, breaks one of the least of these commandments and teaches others to do likewise shall be called the least in the kingdom of heaven. But whoever does and teaches them shall be called great in the kingdom of heaven.

—MATTHEW 5:19

But Zacchaeus stood and said to the Lord, "Look, Lord, I give half of my possessions to the poor. And if I have taken anything from anyone by false accusation, I will repay him four times as much." Jesus said to him, "Today salvation has come to this house, because he also is a son of Abraham.

—LUKE 19:8–9

Beloved, do not avenge yourselves, but rather give place to God's wrath, for it is written: "Vengeance is Mine. I will repay," says the Lord.

—ROMANS 12:19

RIGHTEOUS LIVING

Blessed are those who hunger and thirst for righteousness, for they shall be filled.

—MATTHEW 5:6

But seek first the kingdom of God and His righteousness, and all these things shall be given to you.

—MATTHEW 6:33

To be carnally minded is death, but to be spiritually minded is life and peace.

—ROMANS 8:6

I am confident of this very thing, that He who began a good work in you will perfect it until the day of Jesus Christ.

—PHILIPPIANS 1:6

If you then were raised with Christ, desire those things which are above, where Christ sits at the right hand of God. Set your affection on things above, not on things on earth.

—COLOSSIANS 3:1–2

Study to show yourself approved by God, a workman who need not be ashamed, rightly dividing the word of truth.

—2 Timothy 2:15

SATISFACTION

With long life I will satisfy him and show him My salvation.

—Psalm 91:16

Bless the Lord, O my soul, and all that is within me, bless His holy name. Bless the Lord, O my soul, and forget not all His benefits, who forgives all your iniquities, who heals all your diseases, who redeems your life from the pit, who crowns you with lovingkindness and tender mercies, who satisfies your mouth with good things, so that your youth is renewed like the eagle's.

—Psalm 103:1–5

And the Lord shall guide you continually, and satisfy your soul in drought, and strengthen your bones; and you shall be like a watered garden, and like a spring of water, whose waters do not fail.

—Isaiah 58:11

Jesus said to them, "I am the bread of life. Whoever comes to Me shall never hunger, and whoever believes in Me shall never thirst."

—John 6:35

In Him we have redemption through His blood and the forgiveness of sins according to the riches of His grace.

—Ephesians 1:7

Now faith is the substance of things hoped for, the evidence of things not seen.

—Hebrews 11:1

SEEKING GOD

The Lord is good to those who wait for Him, to the soul that seeks Him.

—Lamentations 3:25

Sow to yourselves righteousness, reap mercy, break up your fallow ground; for it is time to seek the Lord, until He comes and rains righteousness upon you.

—Hosea 10:12

Indeed, thus says the Lord to the house of Israel: Seek Me and live!

—Amos 5:4

That they should seek the Lord so perhaps they might reach for Him and find Him, though He is not far from each one of us.

—Acts 17:27

And without faith it is impossible to please God, for he who comes to God must believe that He exists and that He is a rewarder of those who diligently seek Him.

—Hebrews 11:6

SELF-CONTROL

A fool utters all his mind, but a wise man keeps it in until afterwards.

—Proverbs 29:11

But I bring and keep my body under subjection, lest when preaching to others I myself should be disqualified.

—1 Corinthians 9:27

Put on the whole armor of God that you may be able to stand against the schemes of the devil. For our fight is not against flesh and blood, but against principalities, against powers, against the rulers of the darkness of this world, and against spiritual forces of evil in the heavenly places.

—Ephesians 6:11–12

But refuse profane and foolish myths. Instead, exercise in the ways of godliness. For bodily exercise profits a little, but godliness is profitable in all things, holding promise for the present life and also for the life to come.

—1 Timothy 4:7–8

For this reason make every effort to add virtue to your faith; and to your virtue, knowledge; and to your knowledge, self-control; and to your self-control, patient endurance; and to your patient endurance, godliness; and to your godliness, brotherly kindness; and to your brotherly kindness, love. For if these things reside in you and abound, they ensure that you will neither be useless nor unfruitful in the knowledge of our Lord Jesus Christ.

—2 Peter 1:5–8

SELF-DENIAL

But I say to you, do not resist an evil person. But whoever strikes you on your right cheek, turn to him the other as well. And if anyone sues you in a court of law and takes away your tunic, let him have your cloak also. And whoever compels you to go a mile, go with him two.

—Matthew 5:39–41

Then Jesus said to His disciples, "If anyone will come after Me, let him deny himself, and take up his cross, and follow Me. For whoever would save his life will lose it, and whoever loses his life for My sake will find it. For what will it profit a man if he gains the whole world and loses his own soul? Or what shall a man give in exchange for his soul?

—Matthew 16:24–26

Therefore, brothers, we are debtors not to the flesh, to live according to the flesh. For if you live according to the flesh, you will die, but if through the Spirit you put to death the deeds of the body, you will live.

—Romans 8:12–13

Those who are Christ's have crucified the flesh with its passions and lusts.

—Galatians 5:24

For the grace of God that brings salvation has appeared to all men, teaching us that, denying ungodliness and worldly desires, we should live soberly, righteously, and in godliness in this present world.

—Titus 2:11–12

SELF-ESTEEM

So God created man in His own image; in the image of God He created him; male and female He created them.

—Genesis 1:27

You brought my inner parts into being; You wove me in my mother's womb. I will praise you, for You made me with fear and wonder; marvelous are Your works, and You know me completely.

—Psalm 139:13–14

For I say, through the grace given to me, to everyone among you, not to think of himself more highly than he ought to think, but to think with sound judgment, according to the measure of faith God has distributed to every man.

—Romans 12:3

Therefore do not throw away your confidence, which will be greatly rewarded. For you need patience, so that after you have done the will of God, you will receive the promise.

—Hebrews 10:35–36

Do not let your adorning be the outward adorning of braiding the hair, wearing gold, or putting on fine clothing. But let it be the hidden nature of the heart, that which is not corruptible, even the ornament of a gentle and quiet spirit, which is very precious in the sight of God.

—1 Peter 3:3–4

SELF-IMAGE

For the Lord will be your confidence, and will keep your foot from being caught.

—Proverbs 3:26

For as he thinks in his heart, so is he.

—Proverbs 23:7

I am the vine, you are the branches. He who remains in Me, and I in him, bears much fruit. For without Me you can do nothing.

—John 15:5

I have spoken these things to you, that My joy may remain in you, and that your joy may be full.

—John 15:11

For those whom He foreknew, He predestined to be conformed to the image of His Son, so that He might be the firstborn among many brothers.

—Romans 8:29

For we are His workmanship, created in Christ Jesus for good works, which God prepared beforehand, so that we should walk in them.

—Ephesians 2:10

SELF-RIGHTEOUSNESS

He who is of a proud heart stirs up strife, but he who puts his trust in the Lord will prosper. He who trusts in his own heart is a fool, but whoever walks wisely will be delivered.

—Proverbs 28:25–26

But we all are as an unclean thing, and all our righteousness is as filthy rags; and we all fade as a leaf, and our iniquities, like the wind, have taken us away.

—Isaiah 64:6

Yet you say, "Because I am innocent, surely His anger shall turn away from me." Now I will plead with you, because you say, "I have not sinned."

—Jeremiah 2:35

He said to them, "You are those who justify yourselves before men, but God knows your hearts. For that which is highly esteemed before men is an abomination before God.

—Luke 16:15

Jesus said, "If you were blind, you would have no sin. But now you say, 'We see.' Therefore your sin remains."

—John 9:41

SELF-WORTH

What is man that You are mindful of him, and the son of man that You attend to him? For You have made him a little lower than the angels, and crowned him with glory and honor. You have given him dominion over the works of Your hands; You have put all things under his feet.

—Psalm 8:4–6

You brought my inner parts into being; You wove me in my mother's womb. I will praise you, for You made me with fear and wonder; marvelous are Your works, and You know me completely.

—Psalm 139:13–14

Before I formed you in the womb I knew you; and before you were born I sanctified you, and I ordained you a prophet to the nations.

—Jeremiah 1:5

Are not two sparrows sold for a penny? And not one of them will fall to the ground without your Father. But the very hairs of your head are all numbered. Therefore do not fear. You are more valuable than many sparrows.

—Matthew 10:29–31

"For in Him we live and move and have our being." As some of your own poets have said, "We are His offspring."

—Acts 17:28

Do not be conformed to this world, but be transformed by the renewing of your mind, that you may prove what is the good and acceptable and perfect will of God.

—Romans 12:2

SERVANTHOOD

If it is displeasing to you to serve the Lord, then choose today whom you will serve, if it should be the gods your fathers served beyond the River or the gods of the Amorites' land where you are now living. Yet as for me and my house, we will serve the Lord.

—Joshua 24:15

Fear the Lord; serve Him in truth with all your heart, and consider what great things He has done for you.

—1 Samuel 12:24

But it shall not be so among you. Whoever would be great among you must be your servant, and whoever among you would be greatest must be servant of all.

—Mark 10:43–44

But you are not so. Instead, let him who is greatest among you be as the younger, and he who rules as he who serves. For who is greater: he who sits at the table, or he who serves? Is it not he who sits at the table? But I am among you as He who serves.

—Luke 22:26–27

He who loves his life will lose it. And he who hates his life in this world will keep it for eternal life. If anyone serves Me, he must follow Me. Where I am, there will My servant be also. If anyone serves Me, the Father will honor him.

—John 12:25–26

SERVING GOD

You must follow after the Lord your God, fear Him, and keep His commandments, obey His voice, and you must serve Him, and cling to Him.

—Deuteronomy 13:4

I urge you therefore, brothers, by the mercies of God, that you present your bodies as a living sacrifice, holy, and acceptable to God, which is your reasonable service of worship

—Romans 12:1

Therefore, my beloved brothers, be steadfast, unmovable, always abounding in the work of the Lord, knowing that your labor in the Lord is not in vain.

—1 Corinthians 15:58

And whatever you do, do it heartily, as for the Lord and not for men, knowing that from the Lord you will receive the reward of the inheritance. For you serve the Lord Christ.

—Colossians 3:23–24

But you are a chosen race, a royal priesthood, a holy nation, a people for God's own possession, so that you may declare the goodness of Him who has called you out of darkness into His marvelous light.

—1 Peter 2:9

SEXUAL INTIMACY

Therefore a man will leave his father and his mother and be joined to his wife, and they will become one flesh.

—Genesis 2:24

What? Do you not know that your body is the temple of the Holy Spirit, who is in you, whom you have received from God, and that you are not your own? You were bought with a price. Therefore glorify God in your body and in your spirit, which are God's.

—1 Corinthians 6:19–20

The wife does not have authority over her own body, but the husband does. Likewise, the husband does not have authority over his own body, but the wife does. Do not deprive one another except with consent for a time, that you may give yourselves to fasting and prayer. Then come together again, so that Satan does not tempt you for lack of self-control.

—1 Corinthians 7:4–5

In this way men ought to love their wives as their own bodies. He who loves his wife loves himself. For no one ever hated his own flesh, but nourishes and cherishes it, just as the Lord cares for the church.

—Ephesians 5:28–29

Now the works of the flesh are revealed, which are these: adultery, sexual immorality, impurity, lewdness…envy, murders, drunkenness, carousing, and the like. I warn you, as I previously warned you, that those who do such things shall not inherit the kingdom of God.

—Galatians 5:19–21

Marriage is to be honored among everyone, and the bed undefiled. But God will judge the sexually immoral and adulterers.

—Hebrews 13:4

SINCERITY

If I speak with the tongues of men and of angels, and have not love, I have become as sounding brass or a clanging cymbal. If I have the gift of prophecy, and understand all mysteries and all knowledge, and if I have all faith, so that I could remove mountains, and have not love, I am nothing. If I give all my goods to feed the poor, and if I give my body to be burned, and have not love, it profits me nothing.

—1 Corinthians 13:1–3

For we are not as many are who peddle the word of God. Instead, being sent by God, we sincerely speak in Christ in the sight of God.

—2 Corinthians 2:17

Let the word of Christ dwell in you richly in all wisdom, teaching and admonishing one another in psalms and hymns and spiritual songs, singing with grace in your hearts to the Lord.

—Colossians 3:16

In all things presenting yourself as an example of good works: in doctrine showing integrity, gravity, incorruptibility.

—Titus 2:7

Not by works of righteousness which we have done, but according to His mercy He saved us, through the washing of rebirth and the renewal of the Holy Spirit.

—Titus 3:5

And without faith it is impossible to please God, for he who comes to God must believe that He exists and that He is a rewarder of those who diligently seek Him.

—Hebrews 11:6

SINGLE PARENTING

The Lord, He goes before you. He will be with you. He will not fail you nor forsake you. Do not fear, nor be dismayed.

—Deuteronomy 31:8

No man will be able to stand against you all the days of your life. As I was with Moses, I will be with you. I will not abandon you. I will not leave you.

—Joshua 1:5

My eyes shall be favorable to the faithful in the land, that they may live with me; he who walks in a blameless manner, he shall serve me.

—Psalm 101:6

They said, "Believe in the Lord Jesus Christ, and you and your household will be saved."

—Acts 16:31

Let your lives be without love of money, and be content with the things you have. For He has said: "I will never leave you, nor forsake you."

—Hebrews 13:5

SLANDER

He will bring forth your righteousness as the light, and your judgment as the noonday.

—Psalm 37:6

He will send from heaven and save me from the taunt of the one who crushes me. Selah. God will send forth His mercy and His truth.

—Psalm 57:3

Listen to Me, you who know righteousness, the people in whose heart is My law; do not fear the reproach of men nor be afraid of their revilings.

—Isaiah 51:7

Blessed are you when men revile you, and persecute you, and say all kinds of evil against you falsely for My sake. Rejoice and be very glad, because great is your reward in heaven, for in this manner they persecuted the prophets who were before you.

—Matthew 5:11–12

You will be hated by all men for My name's sake. But he who endures to the end will be saved.

—Matthew 10:22

If you are reproached because of the name of Christ, you are blessed, because the Spirit of glory and of God rests upon you. On their part He is blasphemed, but on your part He is glorified.

—1 Peter 4:14

SPIRITUAL GROWTH

Blessed is the man who walks not in the counsel of the ungodly, nor stands in the path of sinners, nor sits in the seat of scoffers; but his delight is in the law of the Lord, and in His law he meditates day and night. He will be like a tree planted by the rivers of water, that brings forth its fruit in its season; its leaf will not wither, and whatever he does will prosper.

—Psalm 1:1–3

But whoever drinks of the water that I shall give him will never thirst. Indeed, the water that I shall give him will become in him a well of water springing up into eternal life.

—John 4:14

But, speaking the truth in love, we may grow up in all things into Him, who is the head, Christ Himself, from whom the whole body is joined together and connected by every joint and ligament, as every part effectively does its work and grows, building itself up in love.

—Ephesians 4:15–16

For this reason we also, since the day we heard it, do not cease to pray for you and to ask that you may be filled with the knowledge of His will in all wisdom and spiritual understanding; that you may walk in a manner worthy of the Lord, pleasing to all, being fruitful in every good work, and increasing in the knowledge of God.

—Colossians 1:9–10

But grow in the grace and knowledge of our Lord and Savior Jesus Christ. To Him be glory, both now and forever. Amen.

—2 Peter 3:18

STABILITY

He also brought me up out of a horrible pit, out of the miry clay, and set my feet on a rock, and established my steps.

—Psalm 40:2

The wicked flee when no man pursues, but the righteous are bold as a lion. Because of the transgression of a land, many are its princes; but by a man of understanding and knowledge, it shall be prolonged.

—Proverbs 28:1–2

Therefore we should be more attentive to what we have heard, lest we drift away.

—Hebrews 2:1

Therefore, since we are receiving a kingdom that cannot be moved, let us be gracious, by which we may serve God acceptably with reverence and godly fear.

—Hebrews 12:28

If any of you lacks wisdom, let him ask of God, who gives to all men liberally and without criticism, and it will be given to him. But let him ask in faith, without wavering. For he who wavers is like a wave of the sea, driven and tossed with the wind.

—James 1:5–6

Whoever loves his brother lives in the light, and in him there is no cause for stumbling.

—1 John 2:10

STANDING AGAINST WORLDLINESS

If you were of the world, the world would love you as its own. But because you are not of the world, since I chose you out of the world, the world therefore hates you.

—John 15:19

Do not be conformed to this world, but be transformed by the renewing of your mind, that you may prove what is the good and acceptable and perfect will of God.

—Romans 12:2

Set your affection on things above, not on things on earth.

—Colossians 3:2

Teaching us that, denying ungodliness and worldly desires, we should live soberly, righteously, and in godliness in this present world.

—Titus 2:12

Do not love the world or the things in the world. If anyone loves the world, the love of the Father is not in him. For all that is in the world—the lust of the flesh, the lust of the eyes, and the pride of life—is not of the Father, but is of the world. The world and its desires are passing away, but the one who does the will of God lives forever.

—1 John 2:15–17

STRENGTH

Riches and honor flow from You, and You rule over all. In Your hand are power and might, and in Your hand it is to make great and to strengthen all.

—1 Chronicles 29:12

Surely, one shall say, "Only in the Lord are righteousness and strength." Men shall come to him, and all who are incensed at Him shall be ashamed.

—Isaiah 45:24

I will make them strong in the Lord, and they will go to and fro in His name, says the Lord.

—ZECHARIAH 10:12

But He said to me, "My grace is sufficient for you, for My strength is made perfect in weakness." Therefore most gladly I will boast in my weaknesses, that the power of Christ may rest upon me. So I take pleasure in weaknesses, in reproaches, in hardships, in persecutions, and in distresses for Christ's sake. For when I am weak, then I am strong.

—2 CORINTHIANS 12:9–10

Finally, my brothers, be strong in the Lord and in the power of His might.

—EPHESIANS 6:10

STRESS

Cast your burden on the Lord, and He will sustain you; He will never allow the righteous to be moved.

—PSALM 55:22

Heaviness in the heart of man makes it droop, but a good word makes it glad.

—PROVERBS 12:25

For thus says the Lord GOD, the Holy One of Israel: In returning and rest you shall be saved; in quietness and in confidence shall be your strength.

—ISAIAH 30:15

The Lord God is my strength; He will make my feet like hinds' feet, and He will make me walk on my high places.

—Habakkuk 3:19

"Come to Me, all you who labor and are heavily burdened, and I will give you rest. Take My yoke upon you, and learn from Me. For I am meek and lowly in heart, and you will find rest for your souls. For My yoke is easy, and My burden is light."

—Matthew 11:28–30

TAKING AWAY FEAR

Be strong and of a good courage. Fear not, nor be afraid of them, for the Lord your God, it is He who goes with you. He will not fail you, nor forsake you.

—Deuteronomy 31:6

The Lord is my light and my salvation; whom will I fear? The Lord is the strength of my life; of whom will I be afraid?

—Psalm 27:1

Do not be afraid of sudden terror, nor of trouble from the wicked when it comes; for the Lord will be your confidence, and will keep your foot from being caught.

—Proverbs 3:25–26

In righteousness you shall be established; you shall be far from oppression, for you shall not fear, and from terror, for it shall not come near you.

—Isaiah 54:14

There is no fear in love, but perfect love casts out fear, because fear has to do with punishment. Whoever fears is not perfect in love.

—1 John 4:18

TEMPTATION

My son, if sinners entice you, do not consent.

—Proverbs 1:10

Watch and pray that you enter not into temptation. The spirit indeed is willing, but the flesh is weak.

—Matthew 26:41

When He came there, He said to them, "Pray that you may not fall into temptation."

—Luke 22:40

Put on the whole armor of God that you may be able to stand against the schemes of the devil. For our fight is not against flesh and blood, but against principalities, against powers, against the rulers of the darkness of this world, and against spiritual forces of evil in the heavenly places.

—Ephesians 6:11–12

For we do not have a High Priest who cannot sympathize with our weaknesses, but One who was in every sense tempted like we are, yet without sin.

—Hebrews 4:15

THANKFULNESS

The Lord is my strength and my shield; my heart trusted in Him, and I was helped; therefore my heart rejoices, and with my song I will thank Him.

—Psalm 28:7

Now thanks be to God who always causes us to triumph in Christ and through us reveals the fragrance of His knowledge in every place.

—2 Corinthians 2:14

I thank my God for every reminder of you. In every prayer of mine for you all, I have always made requests with joy, due to your fellowship in the gospel from the first day until now.

—Philippians 1:3–5

For everything created by God is good, and not to be refused if it is received with thanksgiving.

—1 Timothy 4:4

Therefore, since we are receiving a kingdom that cannot be moved, let us be gracious, by which we may serve God acceptably with reverence and godly fear.

—Hebrews 12:28

TRIALS

Not only so, but we also boast in tribulation, knowing that tribulation produces patience, patience produces character, and character produces hope. And hope does not disappoint, because the love of God is shed abroad in our hearts by the Holy Spirit who has been given to us.

—Romans 5:3–5

For this reason we do not lose heart: Even though our outward man is perishing, yet our inward man is being renewed day by day. Our light affliction, which lasts but for a moment, works for us a far more exceeding and eternal weight of glory, while we do not look at the things which are seen, but at the things which are not seen. For the things which are seen are temporal, but the things which are not seen are eternal.

—2 Corinthians 4:16–18

My brothers, count it all joy when you fall into diverse temptations, knowing that the trying of your faith develops patience. But let patience perfect its work, that you may be perfect and complete, lacking nothing.

—James 1:2–4

Blessed is the man who endures temptation, for when he is tried, he will receive the crown of life, which the Lord has promised to those who love Him.

—James 1:12

Beloved, do not be surprised at the fiery ordeal that is taking place among you to test you, as though some strange thing happened to you. But rejoice insofar as you share in Christ's sufferings, so that you may rejoice and be glad also in the revelation of His glory.

—1 Peter 4:12–13

TROUBLE

The Lord is my pillar, and my fortress, and my deliverer; my God, my rock, in whom I take refuge; my shield, and the horn of my salvation, my high tower. I will call on the Lord, who is worthy to be praised, and I will be saved from my enemies.

—Psalm 18:2–3

For in the time of trouble He will hide me in His pavilion; in the shelter of His tabernacle He will hide me; He will set me up on a rock.

—Psalm 27:5

Cast your burden on the Lord, and He will sustain you; He will never allow the righteous to be moved.

—Psalm 55:22

The righteous is delivered out of trouble, and the wicked comes in his place.

—Proverbs 11:8

Let not your heart be troubled. You believe in God. Believe also in Me.

—John 14:1

Blessed be God, the Father of our Lord Jesus Christ, the Father of mercies, and the God of all comfort, who comforts us in all our tribulation, that we may be able to comfort those who are in any trouble by the comfort with which we ourselves are comforted by God.

—2 Corinthians 1:3–4

TRUST

The God of my strength, in whom I will trust; my shield and the horn of my salvation, my fortress and my sanctuary; my Savior, You save me from violence.

—2 Samuel 22:3

To You, O Lord, do I lift up my soul. O my God, I trust in You; may I not be ashamed; may my enemies not triumph over me. Yes, let none who wait on You be ashamed; let them be ashamed who transgress without cause.

—Psalm 25:1–3

Trust in the Lord, and do good; dwell in the land, and practice faithfulness. Delight yourself in the Lord, and He will give you the desires of your heart. Commit your way to the Lord; trust also in Him, and He will bring it to pass.

—Psalm 37:3–5

Trust in the LORD with all your heart, and lean not on your own understanding; in all your ways acknowledge Him, and He will direct your paths.

—PROVERBS 3:5–6

When you pass through waters, I will be with you. And through the rivers, they shall not overflow you. When you walk through the fire, you shall not be burned, nor shall the flame kindle on you.

—ISAIAH 43:2

He did not waver at the promise of God through unbelief, but was strong in faith, giving glory to God, and being fully persuaded that what God had promised, He was able to perform.

—ROMANS 4:20–21

UNBELIEVING SPOUSE

Those who know Your name will put their trust in You, for You, LORD, have not forsaken those who seek You.

—PSALM 9:10

I have been young, and now am old; yet I have not seen the righteous forsaken, nor their offspring begging bread.

—PSALM 37:25

Now to the married I command, not I, but the Lord, do not let the wife depart from her husband. But if she departs, let her remain unmarried or be reconciled to her husband. And do not let the husband divorce his wife.

—1 Corinthians 7:10–11

And if the woman has an unbelieving husband who consents to live with her, she should not divorce him. For the unbelieving husband is sanctified by the wife, and the unbelieving wife is sanctified by the husband. Otherwise, your children would be unclean. But now they are holy.

—1 Corinthians 7:13–14

But if the unbeliever departs, let that one depart. A brother or a sister is not bound in such cases. God has called us to peace. For how do you know, O wife, whether you will save your husband? Or how do you know, O husband, whether you will save your wife?

—1 Corinthians 7:15–16

UNDERSTANDING

The giving of Your words gives light; it grants understanding to the simple.

—Psalm 119:130

When wisdom enters your heart, and knowledge is pleasant to your soul, discretion will preserve you; understanding will keep you, to deliver you from the way of the evil man, from the man who speaks perverse things, from those who leave the paths of uprightness to walk in the ways of darkness.

—Proverbs 2:10–13

He who is slow to wrath is of great understanding, but he who is hasty of spirit exalts folly.

—Proverbs 14:29

He who has knowledge spares his words, and a man of understanding is of an excellent spirit.

—Proverbs 17:27

A fool has no delight in understanding, but in expressing his own heart.

—Proverbs 18:2

Counsel in the heart of man is like deep water, but a man of understanding will draw it out.

—Proverbs 20:5

Let your speech always be with grace, seasoned with salt, that you may know how you should answer everyone.

—Colossians 4:6

UNPARDONABLE SIN

He who is not with Me is against Me, and he who does not gather with Me scatters abroad. Therefore I say to you, all kinds of sin and blasphemy will be forgiven men, but the blasphemy against the Holy Spirit will not be forgiven men.

Whoever speaks a word against the Son of Man will be forgiven. But whoever speaks against the Holy Spirit will not be forgiven, neither in this world, nor in the world to come.

—Matthew 12:31–32

Truly I say to you, all sins will be forgiven the sons of men, and whatever blasphemies they speak.

—Mark 3:28

For it is impossible for those who were once enlightened, who have tasted the heavenly gift, who shared in the Holy Spirit, and have tasted the good word of God and the powers of the age to come, if they fall away, to be renewed once more to repentance, since they again crucify to themselves the Son of God and subject Him to public shame.

—Hebrews 6:4–6

How much more severe a punishment do you suppose he deserves, who has trampled under foot the Son of God, and has regarded the blood of the covenant that sanctified him to be a common thing, and has insulted the Spirit of grace?

—Hebrews 10:29

For if after they have escaped the defilements of the world through the knowledge of the Lord and Savior Jesus Christ, and they are again entangled in them and are overcome, the latter end is worse for them than the beginning.

—2 Peter 2:20

UNSELFISHNESS

A new commandment I give to you, that you love one another, even as I have loved you, that you also love one another.

—John 13:34

Greater love has no man than this: that a man lay down his life for his friends.

—John 15:13

Be devoted to one another with brotherly love; prefer one another in honor.

—Romans 12:10

Let each of you look not only to your own interests, but also to the interests of others.

—Philippians 2:4

Command those who are rich in this world that they not be conceited, nor trust in uncertain riches, but in the living God, who richly gives us all things to enjoy. Command that they do good, that they be rich in good works, generous, willing to share, and laying up in store for themselves a good foundation for the coming age, so that they may take hold of eternal life.

—1 Timothy 6:17–19

VALUES

Blessed is the man who walks not in the counsel of the ungodly, nor stands in the path of sinners, nor sits in the seat of scoffers;

but his delight is in the law of the Lord, and in His law he meditates day and night. He will be like a tree planted by the rivers of water, that brings forth its fruit in its season; its leaf will not wither, and whatever he does will prosper.

—Psalm 1:1–3

So embrace, as the elect of God, holy and beloved, a spirit of mercy, kindness, humbleness of mind, meekness, and long-suffering. Bear with one another and forgive one another. If anyone has a quarrel against anyone, even as Christ forgave you, so you must do. And above all these things, embrace love, which is the bond of perfection.

—Colossians 3:12–14

Remembering without ceasing your work of faith, labor of love, and patient hope in our Lord Jesus Christ in the sight of God and our Father.

—1 Thessalonians 1:3

For bodily exercise profits a little, but godliness is profitable in all things, holding promise for the present life and also for the life to come.

—1 Timothy 4:8

Pursue peace with all men, and the holiness without which no one will see the Lord, watching diligently so that no one falls short of the grace of God, lest any root of bitterness spring up to cause trouble, and many become defiled by it.

—Hebrews 12:14–15

WAITING ON THE PROMISE

Wait on the LORD; be strong, and may your heart be stout; wait on the LORD.

—PSALM 27:14

Rest in the LORD, and wait patiently for Him; do not fret because of those who prosper in their way, because of those who make wicked schemes.

—PSALM 37:7

Now, Lord, what do I wait for? My hope is in You.

—PSALM 39:7

But those who wait upon the LORD shall renew their strength; they shall mount up with wings as eagles, they shall run and not be weary, and they shall walk and not faint.

—ISAIAH 40:31

But as for me, I watch for the LORD; I await the God of my salvation; my God will hear me.

—MICAH 7:7

For the vision is yet for an appointed time; but it speaks of the end, and does not lie. If it delays, wait for it; it will surely come, it will not delay.

—HABAKKUK 2:3

WALKING IN GOD'S WAYS

For I will pour water on him who is thirsty, and floods on the dry ground; I will pour out My Spirit on your descendants, and My blessing on your offspring.

—ISAIAH 44:3

But this thing I commanded them, saying, "Obey My voice, and I will be your God, and you shall be My people. And walk in all the ways that I have commanded you, that it may be well with you."

—JEREMIAH 7:23

Bring all the tithes into the storehouse, that there may be food in My house, and test Me now in this, says the LORD of Hosts, if I will not open for you the windows of heaven and pour out for you a blessing, that there will not be room enough to receive it.

—MALACHI 3:10

Heal the sick, cleanse the lepers, raise the dead, and cast out demons. Freely you have received, freely give.

—MATTHEW 10:8

Give, and it will be given to you: Good measure, pressed down, shaken together, and running over will men give unto you. For with the measure you use, it will be measured unto you.

—LUKE 6:38

WEALTH

But you must remember the LORD your God, for it is He who gives you the ability to get wealth, so that He may establish His covenant which He swore to your fathers, as it is today.

—DEUTERONOMY 8:18

A good man leaves an inheritance to his children's children, and the wealth of the sinner is laid up for the just.

—PROVERBS 13:22

The rich rules over the poor, and the borrower is servant to the lender.

—PROVERBS 22:7

Do not store up for yourselves treasures on earth where moth and rust destroy and where thieves break in and steal. But store up for yourselves treasures in heaven, where neither moth nor rust destroy and where thieves do not break in nor steal, for where your treasure is, there will your heart be also.

—MATTHEW 6:19–21

For the love of money is the root of all evil. While coveting after money, some have strayed from the faith and pierced themselves through with many sorrows.

—1 TIMOTHY 6:10

WIDOWS

You shall not afflict any widow or orphan. If you afflict them in any way and they cry at all to Me, I will surely hear their cry. And My anger will burn, and I will kill you with the sword, and your wives will become widows, and your children fatherless.

—Exodus 22:22–24

A father of the fatherless, and a protector of the widows, is God in His holy habitation.

—Psalm 68:5

Learn to do good; seek justice, relieve the oppressed; judge the fatherless, plead for the widow.

—Isaiah 1:17

Do not oppress the widow, orphan, sojourner, or poor. And let none of you contemplate evil deeds in your hearts against his brother.

—Zechariah 7:10

Honor widows that are widows indeed. But if any widow has children or grandchildren, let them learn first to show piety at home and to repay their parents. For this is good and acceptable before God. Now she who is a widow indeed, and desolate, trusts in God, and continues in supplications and prayers night and day. But she who lives in pleasure is dead while she lives.

—1 Timothy 5:3–6

WILL OF GOD

Make me to know Your ways, O Lord; teach me Your paths. Lead me in Your truth and teach me, for You are the God of my salvation; on You I wait all the day.

—Psalm 25:4–5

I will instruct you and teach you in the way which you will go; I will counsel you with my eye on you. Do not be as the horse or as the mule that are without understanding, that must be restrained with bit and bridle, or they will not come near you.

—Psalm 32:8–9

Commit your works to the Lord, and your thoughts will be established.

—Proverbs 16:3

Not everyone who says to Me, "Lord, Lord," shall enter the kingdom of heaven, but he who does the will of My Father who is in heaven.

—Matthew 7:21

"If you love Me, keep My commandments."…Jesus answered him, "If a man loves Me, he will keep My word. My Father will love him, and We will come to him, and make Our home with him.

—John 14:15–23

In everything give thanks, for this is the will of God in Christ Jesus concerning you.

—1 Thessalonians 5:18

WISDOM

To man He said: "Look, the fear of the Lord, that is wisdom; and to depart from evil is understanding."

—Job 28:28

The fear of the Lord is the beginning of wisdom; all who live it have insight. His praise endures forever!

—Psalm 111:10

I have taught you in the way of wisdom; I have led you in right paths. When you walk, your steps will not be hindered, and when you run, you will not stumble.

—Proverbs 4:11–12

For to a man who is pleasing before Him, God gives wisdom, knowledge, and joy; but to the sinner He gives the work of gathering and collecting to give him who is pleasing before God. Also this is vanity and chasing the wind.

—Ecclesiastes 2:26

Whoever hears these sayings of Mine and does them, I will liken him to a wise man who built his house on a rock. And the rain descended, the floods came, and the winds blew and beat on that house. And it did not fall, for it was founded a rock.

—Matthew 7:24–25

WITNESSING

Go therefore and make disciples of all nations, baptizing them in the name of the Father and of the Son and of the Holy Spirit, teaching them to observe all things I have commanded you. And remember, I am with you always, even to the end of the age.

—Matthew 28:19–20

He said to them, "Go into all the world, and preach the gospel to every creature. He who believes and is baptized will be saved. But he who does not believe will be condemned."

—Mark 16:15–16

Yet to all who received Him, He gave the power to become sons of God, to those who believed in His name.

—John 1:12

For I am not ashamed of the gospel of Christ. For it is the power of God for salvation to everyone who believes, to the Jew first, and also to the Greek

—Romans 1:16

I ask you also, true companion, help those women who labored with me in the gospel, with Clement also, and with my other fellow laborers, whose names are in the Book of Life.

—Philippians 4:3

But be self-controlled in all things, endure afflictions, do the work of an evangelist, and prove your ministry.

—2 Timothy 4:5

In this is love: not that we loved God, but that He loved us and sent His Son to be the atoning sacrifice for our sins.

—1 John 4:10

WIVES

Every wise woman builds her house, but the foolish pulls it down with her hands.

—Proverbs 14:1

Who can find a virtuous woman? For her worth is far above rubies.

—Proverbs 31:10

But I say to you that whoever divorces his wife, except for marital unfaithfulness, causes her to commit adultery. And whoever marries her who is divorced commits adultery.

—Matthew 5:32

Wives, be submissive to your own husbands as unto the Lord.

—Ephesians 5:22

Likewise you wives, be submissive to your own husbands, so that if any do not obey the word, they may be won without a word by the conduct of their wives, as they see the purity and reverence of your lives. Do not let your adorning be the outward adorning of braiding the hair, wearing gold, or putting on fine clothing. But let it be the hidden nature of the heart, that which is not corruptible, even the ornament of a gentle and quiet spirit, which is very precious in the sight of God. For in this manner, in the old times, the holy women, who trusted in God, adorned themselves, being submissive to their own husbands.

—1 Peter 3:1–5

WORRY

God is our refuge and strength, a well-proven help in trouble. Therefore we will not fear, though the earth be removed, and though the mountains be carried into the midst of the sea; though its waters roar and foam, though the mountains shake with its swelling. Selah

—Psalm 46:1–3

For he shall be as a tree planted by the waters, and that spreads out its roots by the river, and shall not fear when heat comes, but its leaf shall be green, and it shall not be anxious in the year of drought, neither shall cease from yielding fruit.

—Jeremiah 17:8

Therefore, if God so clothes the grass of the field, which today is here and tomorrow is thrown into the oven, will He not much more clothe you, O you of little faith? Therefore, take no thought, saying, "What shall we eat?" or "What shall we drink?" or "What shall we wear?" (For the Gentiles seek after all these things.) For your heavenly Father knows that you have need of all these things.

—Matthew 6:30–32

Be anxious for nothing, but in everything, by prayer and supplication with gratitude, make your requests known to God. And the peace of God, which surpasses all understanding, will protect your hearts and minds through Christ Jesus.

—Philippians 4:6–7

But let him ask in faith, without wavering. For he who wavers is like a wave of the sea, driven and tossed with the wind.

—James 1:6

WORSHIP

For you shall not worship any other god, for the Lord, whose name is Jealous, is a jealous God.

—Exodus 34:14

I will thank the Lord according to His righteousness, and will sing praise to the name of the Lord Most High.

—Psalm 7:17

O come, let us worship and bow down; let us kneel before the LORD, our Maker. For He is our God, and we are the people of His pasture and the sheep of His hand.

—PSALM 95:6–7

O sing unto the LORD a new song; sing unto the LORD, all the earth!...For the LORD is great, and greatly to be praised; He is to be feared above all gods....Honor and majesty are before Him; strength and beauty are in His sanctuary.

—PSALM 96:1– 6

God is Spirit, and those who worship Him must worship Him in spirit and truth.

—JOHN 4:24

Who shall not fear You, O Lord, and glorify Your name? For You alone are holy. All nations shall come and worship before You, for Your judgments have been revealed.

—REVELATION 15:4